Vander Lúcio Sanches
Alan da Silva Melo
Salete de Matos

Significant Tax Planning

Vander Lúcio Sanches
Alan da Silva Melo
Salete de Matos

Significant Tax Planning

Tax avoidance as a business management alternative

ScienciaScripts

Imprint

Cover image: www.ingimage.com

This book is a translation from the original published under ISBN 978-613-9-63963-2.

Publisher:
Sciencia Scripts
is a trademark of
Dodo Books Indian Ocean Ltd. and OmniScriptum S.R.L publishing group

120 High Road, East Finchley, London, N2 9ED, United Kingdom
Str. Armeneasca 28/1, office 1, Chisinau MD-2012, Republic of Moldova, Europe
Printed at: see last page
ISBN: 978-620-7-71502-2

SUMMARY

In a world of such fierce competition, tax planning, also known as tax avoidance, plays an extremely important role for companies. If taxpayers want to reduce their tax burden, they can do so in two ways. The legal way is called tax planning (tax avoidance or legal savings) and the illegal way is called tax evasion. Tax planning is a set of legal systems aimed at reducing tax payments. Taxpayers have the right to structure their business in the way that best suits them, seeking to reduce the costs of their enterprise, including taxes. If the form is legal and lawful, the tax authorities must respect it. To put theory into practice, a simulation was carried out at **CIA SIILAS SANCHES S/A.** The focus of this book will be on tax regimes: Real Profit vs Presumed Profit. This study will demonstrate and prove the benefits that a correct framework, together with tax-saving measures, can bring to business management.

SUMMARY

CHAPTER 1

INTRODUCTION

The central theme of this book is tax planning, focusing on tax regimes and seeking the best option for reducing the tax burden to which companies are subject. Brazilian tax legislation is very complex, with numerous laws and constant changes, which makes it difficult for business management to keep up to date and interpret them.

The idea that still prevails today is based on avoiding paying or collecting taxes from the public coffers, as these are one of the biggest costs for companies. Tax planning is a tool whose main objective is to reduce the tax burden, not to eliminate it. The law itself makes it possible to pay less tax, but for this to happen it is up to companies to have trained professionals on their staff.

According to Cândido (2007, p.09), Brazil's high tax burden, which is close to 40 per cent of the Gross Domestic Product (GDP), means that tax planning, aimed at reducing taxes, is no longer an option, but an imperative and unavoidable necessity for individuals and companies.

Also, according to the same author, there are companies that, instead of tax planning, prefer tax evasion (selling without an invoice, etc.) which, in addition to security problems (possibility of denunciation) and control, creates a risk of tax assessment, with heavy fines, interest and monetary restatement of the tax debt, often making it impossible for companies to survive.

Planning is a process, an attitude, a skill, in other words, one of the most important management functions. What guarantees a company's survival and continuity lies not in how decisions are made, but in how they are planned. When you think about tax planning, it's because the share of both costs and expenses related to taxes paid by companies is beginning to jeopardise their continuity. The economic/financial statement capable of showing the amount of taxes is the Profit and Loss Account - DRE, which shows sales revenue and profit, which serves as the basis for calculating taxes. That said, this paper is based on the assumption that there is a way to legally reduce them using tax planning.

There is currently a wide range of short courses in this area to prepare professionals for this, but they must already have certain prerequisites, such as a degree in Accounting, Business Administration, Economics or Law. Most companies that implement tax planning recommend an accountant as a key player in the preparation and execution of tax planning (IBPT, 2009, p.17).

The Accountant is in charge of a series of internal company operations, usually being responsible for multiple controls, reconciliations and tax assessments. They also coordinate internal teams and, at least in principle, know the critical points that can lead to failures in planning. There is no point in excellent tax planning, for example, if the simple routines are being carried out by unmotivated and unqualified people, as part of the tax effort may be lost to errors. To think of tax planning in this way is also to think of a team, commitment, responsibility and constant training, because its success is related to the perfect interpretation of the constant laws published monthly, weekly and even daily (IBPT, 2009, p.32).

This book aims to demonstrate the importance of tax planning through its implementation, using a study of the accounting statements. All companies that can make their choice each year in January should first of all carry out a simulation of previous years to check whether the tax regime in question provides the company with a tax burden in line with the tax-saving options that the state offers its taxpayers. The managers of these companies should ask themselves the following question: what would be the reduction in the amount of tax paid if tax planning were implemented at the beginning of that year?

In order to answer this question, the administrator would rely on the work of an accountant who, when planning his actions, would first survey the accounting statements and reports such as the Trial Balance, Balance Sheet, Quarterly Profit and Loss Statements, the Actual Profit Calculation Book and management reports for calculating the Provision for Doubtful Debtors, the Workers' Food Programme, Depreciation, etc.

The accountant will then list the best ways to save on federal, state and municipal taxes that can be applied to the activities inherent in the company's line of business, which could be providing services, trade or industry.

After surveying the facts that could lead to tax savings, a tax planning simulation should be carried out based on the existing tax regimes in Brazil. To facilitate understanding of the theory, a comparison was then made between the results found, considering tax planning at **CIA SILAS SANCHES S/A.** in order to measure the tax savings resulting from tax planning.

The book is organised as follows: Chapter 1 highlights the National Tax System and, in particular, the definitions of taxes and tributes. At the end, a discussion will be presented on the tax competence of the entities studied in this research, which includes taxes under the competence of the Federal Government.

The next chapter discusses tax planning, its necessity and moves on to a discussion of tax evasion and tax avoidance. Its purpose is to place tax planning in the terms of legality, affirming that it is possible in these terms and emphasising its importance in the context of legal complexity and the constant mutability of tax rules in the Brazilian context. At the end of this chapter, the necessary and permanent analyses that must be carried out within companies in order for tax planning to be carried out will also be presented and briefly commented on. These are Economic-financial analysis; Legal analysis; Tax analysis and Fiscal-accounting analysis.

Chapter 3 discusses the tax regimes (Real Profit, Presumed Profit, with an emphasis on the Real Profit Tax Regime, as this was the focus of the book within Tax Planning.

Also in this chapter, the legal conditions imposed on companies that make this choice will be analysed, taking into account the following topics: Estimated Monthly Income Tax; Legal Entity Information Statement; Legal Entity Obliged to Real Profit; Real Profit Calculation Book; Social Contribution on Net Profit; Real Profit Calculation Provisions; Real Profit Income Tax Deductions and Remuneration of Equity and Dividends.

With specific regard to the deductions allowed for Real Profit Income Tax, we will highlight the Workers' Food Programme - PAT; Audiovisual Activity and Cultural Activity and Funds for the Rights of Children and Adolescents and Sports or Para-sports Activity.

The practice to reinforce the understanding of the theory will take place in Chapter 4, Effects of tax planning at Cia Silas Sanches S/A, which begins with a survey of the reports and accounting statements drawn up in 2017, such as the Trial Balance, Balance Sheet, Quarterly Income Statements, Actual Profit Calculation Book and management reports.

In this context, among the profit and loss accounts, we identified those that could result in tax savings, according to differentiated legal treatment. From this effort, it emerged that the accounts Provision for Doubtful Debts, Interest on Equity and Income Tax Deductions should be considered, given the objectives proposed here.

Finally, in the Final Considerations, in addition to emphasising the tax savings that would have been made if tax planning had been implemented by Cia Silas Sanches S/A, the choice of the Real Profit Tax Regime was identified as the right one, to the detriment of Presumed Profit, and the fact that the remuneration of shareholders would also be higher if interest on equity became the basis of this remuneration, to the detriment of remuneration through the payment of dividends. The payment of interest on equity, used as a deductible expense, would make the profit and taxes levied on it lower.

The results were then compared, with tax planning and without tax planning.

To finalise the study, the tax savings from tax planning were measured.

CHAPTER 2

NATIONAL TAX SYSTEM

The aim of this chapter is to present the composition of the National Tax System, in line with the central objective of the research, which is to analyse ways of saving money when paying taxes. It is necessary to know about taxes and their competences before analysing the savings that can be made by applying tax planning interpretations. Its structure is organised as follows: in the next topic, "The State and the Power to Tax", taxes and specifically taxes and contributions.

2.1 The State and the Power to Tax

As well as being sociable, human beings need to develop in society. In fact, it is not enough for him to socialise with himself, but it is in socialising with his fellow human beings that he achieves the most complete satisfaction of his material and spiritual needs (VALÉRIO, 1978, p.15).

In the Middle Ages, with the rise of feudalism due to the fragmentation of the Roman Empire, the idea of the state was weakened. The feeling of territorial identity lost strength to the bond of vassalage, intertwined with a strong religious sentiment. This ushered in an era of small kingdoms and powerful nobility, mainly due to the population's fragility and need for security in the face of constant disputes over territory. Due to the virtual absence of an administrative machine or public services, taxation at the time was basically a form of exploitation and maintenance of social stratification.

More recently, according to Riani (2009, p.101), government costs are financed by resources raised in a variety of ways. They can be obtained through the issue of currency, bond launches, loans and, above all, taxation. The taxation system will vary according to the peculiarities and certain political, economic and social situations of each country. Even if taxation systems are different, they are still the main mechanism for obtaining public resources in the capitalist system.

Furthermore, in this system, and still according to the author, taxation is an important instrument for promoting economic and social adjustments. The tax system can play different roles, depending on the objectives to be achieved and certain specific situations. The fact is that, regardless of the changes that may be made, tax systems remain the government's main fiscal policy instrument.

2.2 Taxes

The National Tax Code, CTN, in its article 3° , defines a tax as follows: "It is any compulsory pecuniary payment, in currency or whose value can be expressed in it, which does not constitute a sanction for an illegal act, established by law and collected through a fully binding administrative activity."

This concept of tax contains the basic rules of the collection system. According to Fabretti (2002, p. 47), these rules are:

• Pecuniary instalment: taxes in general, paid in the normal way and within the normal period for the extinction of the tax obligation, can only be paid in national currency.

• Taxes of other kinds can only be paid in special situations, when authorised by law of the competent federal entity.

• Compulsory: compulsory payment, by the coercive power of the state and independent of the taxpayer's will.

Still with regard to these rules, the collection system does not constitute a sanction for an unlawful act, i.e. the obligation for the taxpayer to pay arises from the practice of a lawful act, i.e. one carried out in accordance with the law (sale of goods, provision of services, etc.) In the case of a tax offence, the penalty will be a fine, which is a sanction for an unlawful act and is not a tax. The fine is not part of tax revenue, but of miscellaneous revenue (Law No. 4.320/64).

The collection system must also be established by law, i.e. taxes can only be instituted or have their rates altered by means of a valid and effective law, in accordance with the principle of legality (art. 150, I, of the Federal Constitution). Finally, the tax must be collected through a fully binding administrative activity: the public administration. Therefore, in order to collect taxes, it is necessary to act in the manner and within the strict limits set by law, otherwise there will be an abuse or misuse of power, which will make the collection liable to annulment.

Also according to Fabretti (2002, p.48), taxes are classified into two types: non-binding taxes and binding taxes. Non-binding taxes - taxes: are those that, once established by law, are due regardless of any state activity in relation to the taxpayer. They are therefore not linked to any specific provision by the state to the taxpayer.

This is a type of tax, defined in art. 16 of the CTN: "Tax is the obligation whose triggering event is a situation independent of any specific state activity relating to the taxpayer."

The tax is a private competence, distributed by the Federal Constitution, i.e. it belongs exclusively to the Union or the States or the Municipalities or the Federal District, according to article 153 of the FC (BRASIL, 1988).

Binding taxes - fees and improvement contributions: these are taxes that, once instituted by law, are only due when there is a state activity provided or made available to the taxpayer.

However, Article 149 of the Federal Constitution, whose tax rules came into force on 1 March 1989, introduced a new type of tax: special contributions. These are currently subdivided into social contributions, contributions to intervene in the economic domain, contributions on professional and economic categories and provisional contributions on financial transactions. However, this new type of tax, which is collected by the Federal Government and is not subject to revenue sharing with the states and municipalities, has been growing and increasingly represents a significant percentage of total federal tax collection.

Non-binding taxes: these are taxes that, once instituted by law, are due regardless of any state activity in relation to the taxpayer.

For Fabretti (2002, p.49), a fee is defined in articles 77 and 78 of the CTN and its taxable event is the regular exercise of police power or the actual or potential use of a specific and divisible public service provided or made available to the taxpayer (article 77). According to Nogueira (1995, p.35), a fee is a tax collected due to the exercise of police power or the actual or potential use of a specific and divisible public service, provided to the taxpayer or made available to them (CTN, art.70). According to Fúhrer and Fúhrer (2003, p.54), the improvement contribution is a tax on the increase in value of private property as a result of public works carried out. Although it has a similar name, it is quite different in nature from other contributions.

According to the above authors, social contributions, also known as special or parafiscal contributions, are taxes designed to raise funds for certain areas of interest to the public authorities, i.e. the social contribution has a certain destination and is collected for a predetermined purpose, indicated in the law that instituted it.

Hack (2008, p.12) explains the concept of tribute defined by the CTN, in its article 3º . "Tribute is any pecuniary instalment (...) in currency or whose value can be expressed in it" - This element shows that tribute is always expressed in money. This means that a tax cannot be paid in sacks of corn or hours of labour. Tax always presupposes payment in money, with a value determined in national currency.

"A tax is any compulsory pecuniary instalment" - here we see that a tax is compulsory. Once the law states that a certain fact gives rise to a tax credit, it must be collected. Therefore, the payment of tax is not optional, but compulsory. Taxes are compulsory by their very nature, and there is no such thing as a voluntary tax. It is possible to make donations to the state, but this does not constitute a tax because it is a voluntary, not compulsory, payment (HACK, 2009, p.13).

According to Hack (2008, p.13), "A tax is any pecuniary payment (...) that does not constitute a sanction for an illegal act" - in order to characterise a tax, it is assumed that it is derived from a lawful activity. Lawful acts are those that are in accordance with the law; they are those that do not contravene legal norms, that obey their precepts. For example, a person who parks their car in the permitted place is doing something that is lawful, i.e. does not contravene the law.

A wrongful act, on the other hand, is one that goes against the law. So, in the same example above, if someone parks in a prohibited place or on the pavement, they are committing an unlawful act. Because it is contrary to the law, an unlawful act must be repressed and therefore presupposes the application of a penalty, a sanction when it occurs. So when an individual parks their car illegally, they are obliged to pay a fine, which is nothing more than a compulsory pecuniary payment laid down by law.

Taxes must be collected by means of a fully binding administrative activity. This element points to the administrative activity involved in tax collection. Binding actions are those in which the law indicates what must be done in a given situation, leaving no room for choice on the part of the agent (HACK, 2008, p.16).

Having seen the concept of tax, we discover the object of study of Tax Law: it is the branch of law that studies taxes and the relationships arising from them. According to Baleeiro (2001, p.05), "Financial Law comprises the set of financial rules - revenue, expenditure, budget, credit and tax procedure".

Fiscal Law, synonymous with Tax Law, is applied contemporaneously and despite any etymological contradiction, to the restricted field of compulsory revenue. It primarily regulates the legal relations between the tax authorities, as the active subject, and the taxpayer or third parties as the passive subjects.

> We mustn't forget, however, that taxation is part of a larger phenomenon related to public finances and the budget. Seen from a financial perspective, the state has income and expenditure. Among the possible revenues is that derived from the collection of taxes; in other words, the tax is part of a larger context in which the state's financial situation is considered, taking into account all its revenues and expenses. These issues are studied by Financial Law, a branch of law dedicated to public finances and the budget. Taxes, however, due to their importance as a major source of resources for the state, are studied in a different branch of Financial Law, as they have their own discipline. This reasoning demonstrates the link between Tax Law and Financial Law. Another strong link between Tax Law is with Administrative Law, which is the branch of legal science dedicated to the study of the State and Public Administration. This branch studies subjects such as administrative acts, administrative tenders and contracts and the discipline of public services. As the very concept of a tax says, it is levied by means of a "fully binding administrative activity", which points to a strong role for the rules of Administrative Law in the tax area (HACK, 2008, p. 17).

According to Nogueira (1995, p.47), the state's right to tax stems from its power of empire, by which it can derive a portion of the assets of the people subject to its jurisdiction into its coffers, which are called "derived revenues" or tributes, divided into taxes, fees and contributions.

According to Campos (1995, p.55), tax law comes from the Latin *tributarius,* who pays tribute, i.e. the law relating to taxes includes the various types of tax.

Carvalho (2000, p.28) teaches that the sources of law will be events in the social world, legalised by rules of the system and accredited to produce legal norms that introduce other norms into the system, whether general and abstract, general and concrete, individual and abstract or individual and concrete.

2.3 Taxes

Carrazza (2002, p.71) teaches that a tax is not linked to state action. This idea, by the way, was very well explained in article 16 of the CTN, which states: "tax is the obligation whose triggering event is a situation independent of any specific state activity, relating to the taxpayer". When imposing a tax, the political entity does not need to carry out any specific state activity in favour of the taxpayer who will be taxed.
support. This type of tax (unlike fees and improvement contributions) does not require any consideration.

The taxes that make up the national tax system are exclusively those listed in this title, with the competences and limitations set out therein (CTN, art. 17). It is incumbent upon I - to the Union, to institute, in the Federal Territories, the taxes attributed to the States and, if they are not divided into Municipalities, cumulatively, those attributed to them; II - to the Federal District and to the States not divided into Municipalities, to institute, cumulatively, the taxes attributed to the States and to the Municipalities (CTN, art. 18, I and II).

Table I below illustrates the main taxes by competent federal level.

TABLE I

Federal: (Union)
Tax on imports - II; Tax on exports - IE; Tax on industrialised products - IPI; Tax on credit, exchange and insurance transactions or transactions relating to securities - IOF; Income tax - IR; Tax on rural property - ITR.

State: (States) Tax on transfers, *causa mortis* and donations - ITCD; Tax on the circulation of goods and on the provision of interstate and intercity transport and communication services - ICMS; Tax on the ownership of motor vehicles - IPVA.
Municipal: (Municipalities) Property tax - IPTU; Tax on the (onerous) *inter vivos* transfer of goods and property - ITBI; Tax on services of any kind - ISS. . The Federal District is responsible for both state and municipal taxes - Art. 32, § 1° . and 147 of the FC and art. 18 of the CTN.

Source: IBPT - Brazilian Institute of Tax Planning

2.4 Taxable event

According to Fabretti (1999, p.40), a taxable event is the realisation of the taxable event provided for in the abstract by law, which generates (gives rise to) the tax obligation.

The triggering event for the main obligation is the situation defined by law as necessary and sufficient for its occurrence (CTN, art. 114).

The triggering event for an ancillary obligation is any situation which, under the applicable legislation, requires the practice or abstention from an act that does not constitute a primary obligation (CTN, art. 115).

Furthermore, unless the law provides otherwise, the triggering event shall be deemed to have occurred and its effects to exist: I - in the case of a factual situation, from the moment when the material circumstances necessary for it to produce the effects that normally pertain to it occur; II - in the case of a legal situation, from the moment when it is definitively constituted, under the terms of the applicable law. (CTN, art. 116, I and II).

Carvalho (1995, p.30) chooses to call it a legal tax event. It is a legal event because it has the power to radiate legal effects. And it is taxable for the simple reason that its effectiveness is directly linked to the imposition of the tax.

CHAPTER 3

TAX PLANNING

The aim of this chapter is to present concepts of tax avoidance, making a distinction between what is considered to be tax planning and what is considered to be tax evasion, which is the taxable person's avoidance of paying taxes. Its structure is organised as follows: Importance and Necessity of Tax Planning, Tax Evasion, and Purposes of Tax Avoidance.

3.1 The Importance and Necessity of Tax Planning

According to Borges (1996, p.55), two factors determine the importance and necessity of tax planning in companies. The first is the high tax burden on the business world. The other is business awareness of the significant degree of complexity, sophistication, alternation and versatility of the relevant legislation. In reality, the effective interaction of these factors in the business context has required the management team of business organisations to invest a great deal of energy and resources in identifying all the legal alternatives available to their transactions and business operations, in order to adopt the one that results in the least onerous tax consequences.

Also according to Borges (1996, p.55), the nature of tax planning consists of organising the company's economic and commercial ventures by using legal structures and forms capable of blocking the hypothesis of tax incidence from materialising, or making it materialise to the extent or at the time that is most conducive to it. This is a technical-functional behaviour, adopted in the business world, which aims to exclude, reduce or postpone the respective tax burdens.

The same author defines tax planning as a management technique that aims to plan industrial operations, commercial businesses and the provision of services in such a way as to enable knowledge of the obligations and tax burdens included in each of the relevant legal alternatives so that, using legitimate means and instruments, the one that enables the cancellation, reduction or postponement of the tax burden can be adopted.

According to Campos (2007, p.11), tax planning is the search for alternatives and a reduction in the tax burden, by lawful means (tax avoidance), before the taxable event occurs.

Although the author mentions other names given to Tax Planning such as: Legitimate Tax Evasion, Tax Avoidance or the Right to Save Taxes, he makes it clear that it doesn't matter which of these expressions is more appropriate to the nature and characteristics of the institute in question. In fact, it is important to clarify that all of them take place in a legal sphere characterised by freedom of action - in other words, the absence of taxation, reduced or postponed taxation - within and over certain limits strictly demarcated by constitutional principles (CAMPOS, 2007).

Proper tax planning must act preventively, seeking to minimise and/or neutralise tax and labour risks, using the following most important mechanisms:

• Be aware of the operations in which the tax credit can be used and deducted in the sales operation (indirect and non-cumulative taxes such as ICMS and IPI);

• All situations in which tax disbursements can be deferred (deferral), which is positive for cash flow;

• Use all expenses incurred and all provisions allowed by the tax authorities to deduct from profit (CAMPOS, 2007).

These cost-cutting factors, in theory, make it possible to reduce prices and, consequently, make the product more competitive on the market.

Prevention leads to tax avoidance and the legal reduction of taxes, while poor planning, which reduces the tax burden illegally, is considered tax evasion and is a tax evasion offence (Law No. 8.137/90).

3.2 Tax evasion

It is characteristic of human beings to try to minimise their tax burden, i.e. the amount of money they have to hand over to the state. Historically, there has been a constant struggle between taxpayers and the tax authorities. Taxpayers are always looking to raise revenue, regardless of the means by which they achieve this end. And the other, seeking to develop procedures aimed at excluding or minimising tax burdens. The situation of non-compliance with the rule (default or underpayment) generates the sanction for the illegal act: the coercive seizure of the monetary value of the tax by the state (AMARAL , 2009, p.58).

According to Dória (1971, p.21), "tax evasion lato sensu is defined as any action or omission aimed at avoiding, reducing or delaying the fulfilment of a tax obligation."

As a prerequisite for the existence of evasion, the doctrine has put forward the cunning will of the taxpayer to delay, reduce or eliminate the payment of tax. Thus, the mere omissive behaviour of the taxpayer is not enough, but a commissive act demonstrating the will to defraud the tax authorities is necessary. In fact, the fraudulent act is just the classic means of evasion.

Dória (1971, p.24) drew up the following classification of tax evasion:

- Omissive evasion (intentional or not);
- Improper evasion (abstention from incidence, economic transfer);
- Unintentional (ignorance of tax duty);
- Commissive evasion (always intentional);

- Illicit (fraud, simulation, collusion);
- Lawful or legitimate (evasion *stricto sensu,* tax avoidance or tax saving).

For him, improper evasion and evasion by inaction are evasions that are generally not more serious, indicating little or no danger on the part of the agent by omission, except in the case of tax evasion.

3.2.1 Illicit Evasion, Tax Evasion or Tax Fraud

Illicit evasion is defined as "the conscious and voluntary action of an individual tending, by illicit means, to eliminate, reduce or delay the payment of tax actually due"

Article 72 of Law No. 4.502/64 states that "fraud is any intentional action or omission aimed at preventing or delaying, in whole or in part, the occurrence of the taxable event of the main tax obligation, or at excluding or modifying its essential characteristics, in order to reduce the amount of tax due, or to defer its payment".

For Machado (2001, p.28), tax evasion refers to the following:

> This definition, taken literally, leads to the patently absurd conclusion that a taxpayer who simply refrains from carrying out an act that would result in a tax liability is engaging in fraudulent and therefore unlawful behaviour. Anyone who stopped earning income would be practising fraud, because they would be preventing the taxable event of the tax on income and earnings of any nature from occurring." In his view, this definition should be understood as preventing or delaying, by means of an artifice, the externalisation of a fact that has actually occurred, or is about to occur, and constitutes the materialisation of a taxable event.

The crime of tax evasion is laid down in Law 4.729/65, art. 1º .
Misappropriation of taxes is also a criminal offence (Law 4.357/64 - art. 11). Decree 325 of 1st November 1991 regulates the reporting to the Federal Public Prosecutor's Office of criminal offences under tax legislation and functional crimes against the tax order. Law 8137 of 27 December 1990 defines crimes against the economic and tax order.

3.3 Purposes of Tax Avoidance

According to Dória (1971), there are three purposes of tax avoidance:

1- avoiding the incidence of the tax: steps are taken to prevent the taxable event from occurring;
2- reduce the amount of tax;
3- delaying payment of the tax.

In the first case, the taxable event is avoided. For example: so that the company doesn't have to pay INSS on the "Pro-Labore" (20%), the partners set a small amount of withdrawals and take most of it out as profits, because as of January 1996, they are not subject to IR either at source or in the tax return.

In order to reduce the amount of tax, steps are taken to reduce the tax rate or the tax base. A commercial company established in Paraná, for example, where most of its sales are state sales (ICMS rate of 18%) can transfer its headquarters to a neighbouring state and then carry out interstate ICMS operations, where the rate is 12%.

Finally, in order to delay payment of the tax, the taxpayer adopts measures designed to postpone (delay) payment of the tax without incurring a fine. This requires the adoption of administrative or judicial measures. If, for example, there is doubt as to the incidence of a certain tax on a transaction, the company can file a tax enquiry, claiming to pay a lower rate and calculate the tax on a lower calculation basis. Until the enquiry is judged, the company can pay the lower amount of tax, thus avoiding a fine.

Also according to Dória (1971), when adopting a tax avoidance system, it is necessary to analyse four aspects:

- Economic and financial analysis: Adopt procedures aimed at maximising the planning result. E.g.: Judicial deposits are often detrimental to the company, because in addition to the cash outflow, the company cannot take advantage of the deductibility of the expense.
- Legal analysis: There must be legal grounds to be argued. As the main taxes are legally questionable, the arguments are plentiful;
- Tax analysis: Be careful not to "call in" the inspectorate. Two constitutional precepts protect the adoption of legal economy: the Principle of Ample Defence and Due Process of Law;
- Tax-accounting analysis: Adopting procedures that allow savings on other taxes, seeking to maximise profit and minimise risk.

CHAPTER 4

TAX REGIMES

The choice of tax regime and its framework will define the incidence and calculation basis of federal taxes. In Brazil, there are three types of tax regime most commonly used by companies, which they can fit into according to their activities.

- Real Profit
- Presumed Profit
- Simples Nacional

Many small and medium-sized companies that have not opted for or are unable to operate under the SIMPLES system and that are within the limit and authorised by law to operate under the Presumed Profit system are in doubt when it comes to choosing which taxation method they will adopt to calculate IRPJ (Corporate Income Tax) and CSLL (Social Contribution on Net Profit). Real Profit or Presumed Profit?

First of all, companies should check whether their activities are included in the list of companies that are not authorised to make Presumed Profits (article 14 of Law 9718/1998, amended by Law 10637/2002) and observe the revenue limit for the previous calendar year. The basis for calculating IRPJ and CSLL will be different in the calculation methods, but the percentages of presumed profit that will be levied on Gross Revenue from economic activity will be the same. By way of example, the percentage of profit that will be levied on Gross Revenue for companies classified as industry or commerce will be 8% for calculating IRPJ and 12% for calculating CSLL.

4.1 Simples Nacional

According to the Federal Revenue Office (BRASIL, 2007), the Integrated System for the Payment of Taxes and Contributions by Micro and Small Businesses (SIMPLES) is a differentiated, simplified and favoured tax regime set out in Supplementary Law 123 of 14 December 2006, applicable to Micro and Small Businesses as of 01 July 2007. As of 2018, the gross revenue limit will be R$4,800,000.00/year. However, for the purposes of paying ICMS and ISS under Simples Nacional, the maximum gross revenue limit will be R$3,600,000.00, which corresponds to an average of R$400,000.00.

4.1.1 New Simples Nacional Tables 2018

To familiarise yourself with the new tables, let's take a look at the five annexes created by Supplementary Law No 155, which amended Supplementary Law No 123. It's worth noting that the number of turnover bands has dropped from 20 to just 6.

First of all, find out which annex your company falls into. The calculation is as follows: total annual revenue for the year multiplied by the indicated rate. Then just deduct the amount indicated and divide the final figure by the total gross annual revenue.

In short: (RBT12*Aliq - PD)/RBT12

- RBT12: Total Gross Revenue accumulated in the previous twelve months
- Aliq: constant nominal rate (Annexes I and V of the Supplementary Law)
- PD: constant deductible portion (Annexes I and V of the Supplementary Law)

Annex I of Simples Nacional 2018

Participants: retail businesses (shops in general)

Total Gross Revenue in 12 months	Rate	How much to deduct from the amount collected
Up to R$ 180,000.00	4%	0
From 180,000.01 to 360,000.00	7,3%	R$ 5.940,00
From 360,000.01 to 720,000.00	9,5%	R$ 13.860,00
From 720,000.01 to 1,800,000.00	10,7%	R$ 22.500,00
From 1,800,000.01 to 3,600,000.00	14,3%	R$ 87.300,00
From 3,600,000.01 to 4,800,000.00	19%	R$ 378.000,00

Annex II of Simples Nacional 2018

Participants: factories/industries and industrial companies

Total Gross Revenue in 12 months	Rate	How much to deduct from the amount collected
Up to R$ 180,000.00	4,5%	0
From 180,000.01 to 360,000.00	7,8%	R$ 5.940,00
From 360,000.01 to 720,000.00	10%	R$ 13.860,00
From 720,000.01 to 1,800,000.00	11,2%	R$ 22.500,00
From 1,800,000.01 to 3,600,000.00	14,7%	R$ 85.500,00
From 3,600,000.01 to 4,800,000.00	30%	R$ 720.000,00

Annex III of Simples Nacional 2018

Participants: companies offering installation, repair and maintenance services. This annex also includes travel agencies, accountancy offices, gyms, laboratories, medical and dental companies (the list in Annex III will be in § 5-B, § 5-D and § 5-F of article 18 of Complementary Law 123).

Total Gross Revenue in 12 months	Rate	How much to deduct from the amount collected
Up to R$ 180,000.00	6%	0
From 180,000.01 to 360,000.00	11,2%	R$ 9.360,00
From 360,000.01 to 720,000.00	13,5%	R$ 17.640,00
From 720,000.01 to 1,800,000.00	16%	R$ 35.640,00
From 1,800,000.01 to 3,600,000.00	21%	R$ 125.640,00
From 3,600,000.01 to 4,800,000.00	33%	R$ 648.000,00

Annex IV of Simples Nacional 2018

Participants: companies that provide cleaning, surveillance, works, building construction, legal services (the list in Annex IV will be in § 5-C of article 18 of Complementary Law 123)

Total Gross Revenue in 12 months	Rate	How much to deduct from the amount collected
Up to R$ 180,000.00	4,5%	0
From 180,000.01 to 360,000.00	9%	R$8.100,00

From 360,000.01 to 720,000.00	10,2%	R$ 12.420,00
From 720,000.01 to 1,800,000.00	14%	R$ 39.780,00
From 1,800,000.01 to 3,600,000.00	22%	R$ 183.780,00
From 3,600,000.01 to 4,800,000.00	33%	R$ 828.000,00

Annex V of Simples Nacional 2018

Participants: companies that provide auditing, journalism, technology, advertising and engineering services, among others (the list in Annex IV will be in § 5-I of article 18 of Complementary Law 123)

Total Gross Revenue in 12 months	Rate	How much to deduct from the amount collected
Up to R$ 180,000.00	15,5%	0
From 180,000.01 to 360,000.00	18%	R$ 4.500,00
From 360,000.01 to 720,000.00	19,5%	R$ 9.900,00
From 720,000.01 to 1,800,000.00	20,5%	R$ 17.100,00
From 1,800,000.01 to 3,600,000.00	23%	R$62.100,00
From 3,600,000.01 to 4,800,000.00	30,50%	R$ 540.000,00

According to Higuchi (2006, p.66), Simples Nacional implies the monthly payment of the following taxes through a single collection document:

- Corporate Income Tax (IRPJ);
- Tax on Industrialised Products (IPI);
- Social Contribution on Net Profit (CSLL);
- Contribution to the Financing of Social Security (COFINS);
- Contribution to the Social Integration Programme (PIS);
- Social Security Contribution (employer's share);
- Tax on Operations Relating to the Circulation of Goods and on the Provision of Interstate and Intermunicipal Transport and Communication Services (ICMS);
- Tax on Services of Any Kind (ISSQN).

All states and municipalities are obliged to participate in Simples Nacional. The tax owed by companies opting for this system is determined by applying the tables in the annexes to LC 123/06. To determine the tax rate, the debtor will use the gross revenue accumulated in the 12 months prior to the calculation period. The amount due each month will result from applying the corresponding rate to the monthly gross revenue earned (HIGUCHI, 2006, p.69).

4.2 Presumed Profit

In this type of tax regime, the amount to be taxed is determined on the basis of gross revenue, by applying variable rates depending on the activity that generates the revenue. Legal entities whose total gross revenue in the previous calendar year was equal to or less than R$ 78,000,000.00 or the proportional limit of R$ 7,500,000.00 multiplied by the number of months of activity in the year, if this is less than 12 months, can opt for presumed profit. Under the presumed profit regime, there are four types of federal tax levied on turnover, including PIS and COFINS, which must be calculated monthly, and IRPJ and CSLL, which must be calculated quarterly (http://www.portaltributario.com.br, 2018).

It can be said that presumed profit is a presumption on the part of the tax authorities of what a company's profit would be if accounting didn't exist. However, we have noticed that some companies have complete bookkeeping, with the rigours of the fundamental rules and principles of accounting, and even so end up opting for taxation based on presumed profit. Most of the time, this is due to a lack of knowledge on the part of the business owners or even the accountants themselves, who are unaware of or have little information about the other forms of taxation. This is where tax planning comes in, which should consciously reduce the tax burden in order to find the best option for the company, be it through real or presumed profit (HIGUCHI, 2006, p.55).

4.3 Real Profit

Legal entities taxed on actual profit may determine profit on the basis of an annual balance sheet drawn up on 31 December or by drawing up quarterly balance sheets in accordance with Law No. 9430/96. Legal entities that fall under any of the clauses of Article 14 of Law No. 9718/98 must be taxed based on real profit. For other legal entities, taxation based on real profit is an option.

Article 1° of Law No. 9.718/98 replaced the calculation of monthly real profit with quarterly profit. It made headlines in the press, saying that corporate income tax had been simplified. There is no such simplification, because well-managed companies have not been calculating the monthly real profit and will not calculate the quarterly real profit (HIGUCHI, 2006, p. 5). In other words, the monthly or quarterly real profit doesn't bring a single advantage, but many disadvantages, such as limiting the offsetting of tax losses and the possibility of committing more tax offences.

In quarterly real profit, the profit from the previous quarter cannot be offset against the tax loss from subsequent quarters, even within the same calendar year. The tax loss from one quarter can only be reduced by up to 30 per cent of the real profit from subsequent quarters. In the case of annual real profit, the company may fully offset losses against profits calculated within the same calendar year.

The Brazilian Federal Revenue Service defines the legal entities obliged to follow this regime:

> - Whose total revenue, i.e. the sum of monthly gross revenue in the previous calendar year, exceeds the limit of R$ **78,000,000.00** (seventy-eight million reais), or R$ **6,500,000.00** (six million five hundred thousand reais) multiplied by the number of months

in the period, when less than twelve months;

- Whose activities are commercial banks, investment banks, development banks, savings banks, credit, financing and investment companies, property credit companies, securities and foreign exchange brokerage companies,

- Securities distributors, leasing companies, credit cooperatives, private insurance and capitalisation companies and open-ended private pension entities;

- Who have profits, income or capital gains from abroad;

- Which, during the calendar year, have made monthly income tax payments, determined on the estimated calculation basis, in accordance with Article 2 of Law No. 9430 of 1996;

- That operate the activities of cumulative and continuous provision of credit, marketing, credit management, selection and risk advisory services, management of accounts payable and receivable, purchases of credit rights resulting from forward sales or the provision of services (factoring) (Receita Federal do Brasil).

4.4 Estimated Monthly Income Tax

According to Higuchi (2006, p.26), legal entities that opt for annual real profit taxation will have to pay monthly income tax and social contribution on profit calculated by estimate. The tax and contribution on the month's operations must be paid by the last working day of the following month. The income tax rate will remain at 15 per cent and the additional tax rate at 10 per cent, but the additional tax will have to be paid monthly on the portion of the estimated profit that exceeds R$20,000.00.

The basis for calculating the income tax to be paid each month is the sum of a percentage applied to the gross revenue for the month, plus capital gains, other income and positive results, with the exception of income or gains taxed as financial investments. The percentages applicable to gross revenue vary according to the activity of the legal entity and are set out in art. 15 of Law no. 9,249/95.

The percentages applicable to gross revenue in determining the basis for calculating income tax are the same both for the payment of estimated monthly tax by legal entities taxed on the basis of annual real profit and for taxation by Presumed Profit, in which the rulings of the Supreme Court are cited.

Internal Revenue Service. The percentages are: 8% on the sale of goods and products; 1.6% on the resale, for consumption, of petroleum-derived fuel, ethyl alcohol and natural gas; 16% on the provision of transport services, except freight, which is 8%; 16% for financial institutions and the like; 16% on the provision of services in general by legal entities with gross revenue of up to R$ 120,000, except hospital services, transport and regulated professions and 32% on the provision of other services (HIGUCHI, 2006, p.26).

IPI does not make up gross revenue and cancelled sales, sales returns and unconditional discounts granted will be excluded from gross revenue. In the case of diversified activities, the percentage corresponding to each activity will be applied. Thus, if the legal entity had revenue from the sale of goods and commission from intermediation, the percentage of 8% will be applied to the former, while the percentage of 32% will be applied to commission revenue (HIGUCHI, 2006, p.26).

The tax calculation bases, which must be determined according to the legislation in force on the date the taxable event occurs, are the Actual Profit, Presumed Profit or Arbitrated Profit, corresponding to the calculation period. The rate for taxable events occurring from 1° January 2006 is 15%, to be applied to the calculation base. In addition to the IRPJ charged at the 15% rate, an additional 10% is levied on the portion of the real, presumed or arbitrated profit that exceeds the amount resulting from multiplying R$ 20,000.00 (twenty thousand reais) by the number of months in the respective calculation period. The deadline for payment is the last working day of the month following the end of the quarter. Despite the legal entity's choice, the tax due can be paid in up to three equal and successive monthly instalments, due on the last working day of the three months following the end of the quarter. None of these instalments may be less than R$1,000.00 and tax of less than R$2,000.00 must be paid in a single instalment (HIGUCHI, 2006, p.27).

4.5 Corporate Information Statement

Legal entities are obliged to file a corporate tax return (formerly an income tax return) in the calendar year following that in which the tax is calculated. Actual Profit is the Result (Profit or Loss) for the assessment period (before computing the provision for income tax), adjusted by the additions, exclusions and offsets prescribed or authorised by the Income Tax legislation. It can be seen immediately that, as the starting point for determining real profit is the net result calculated in the commercial bookkeeping, legal entities taxed on the basis of real profit are obliged to keep the information in good order and safekeeping, with strict observance of commercial and tax laws and generally accepted accounting principles (HIGUCHI, 2006, p.27).

4.5.1 Additions

In determining the actual profit, the expenses deducted in determining the net profit which, according to tax legislation, are not deductible in determining the actual profit, must be added to the net profit for the calculation period, such as:

- social contribution on net profit;
- fines for tax offences, except those of a compensatory nature and those imposed for offences that do not result in non-payment or insufficient payment of taxes or contributions;
- depreciation, amortisation, maintenance, repair, upkeep, taxes, fees, insurance and any other expenditure on movable and immovable property, unless intrinsically related to the production of goods and services;
- leasing and rental of real estate, except when intrinsically related to the production or

commercialisation of goods and services;

- food expenses for partners, shareholders and directors;
- non-compensatory contributions, except those intended to cover insurance, health plans and complementary benefits similar to those of the social security system

in favour of the employees and managers of the legal entity;

- donations, except those made to non-profit educational and research institutions whose creation has been authorised by federal law, up to the limit of 1.5% of operating profit, before deduction, and those made to non-profit civil entities that provide free services for the benefit of employees of the donating legal entity and their dependents, or for the benefit of the community in which they operate, up to the limit of 2% of operating profit, before deduction, and those made to projects of a cultural nature, approved by the National Culture Commission;
- amortisation of goodwill on the acquisition of equity holdings subject to equity valuation, the amount of which must be recorded in part "B" of the Real Profit Calculation Book, Lalur, to be computed in real profit in the period in which the sale or liquidation of the investment occurs;
- the loss on the sale or write-off of investments acquired through a tax incentive to deduct income tax;
- losses arising from unsettled credits, which have been computed in the income statement without observing the limits set out in the legislation;
- losses on the receipt of credits with a controlling, controlled, affiliated or interconnected legal entity, or with an individual who is a controlling shareholder, partner, owner or manager of the creditor legal entity or a relative up to the third degree;
- the indirect remuneration of partners, directors or administrators, when the beneficiary is not identified, as well as the income tax levied at source on this remuneration;
- the negative result of a holding company, the value of non-deductible provisions, except for the following:
    - provision for holiday pay and Christmas bonus;
    - technical provisions of insurance and capitalisation companies, as well as private pension entities, whose constitution is required by the special legislation applicable to them (HIGUCHI, 2006, p.28).

4.6 Legal Entities obliged to make Real Profit

Legal entities whose total revenue, i.e. the sum of monthly gross revenue, other revenue and capital gains, net gains from operations in the variable income markets and nominal income from fixed income financial investments, in the previous calendar year, exceeds the limit of R$ 78,000,000.00 (seventy-eight million reais), or above R$ 6,500,000.00 (six million five hundred thousand reais) multiplied by the number of months in the period, are obliged to be taxed on the basis of real profit.000,000.00 (seventy-eight million reais), or more than R$ 6,500,000.00 (six million five hundred thousand reais) multiplied by the number of months in the period, when less than twelve months. (http://www.portaltributario.com.br, 2018)

Table II below illustrates the activities and the percentages that should be applied to the estimated IRPJ calculation base.

TABLE II

Determining the Estimated IRPJ Calculation Basis	
ACTIVITY	%
- Resale for consumption of fuels derived from petroleum, ethyl alcohol and natural gas	1.6
- Sale of goods - Hospital services - Sale of own manufactured products or industrialisation to order - Real estate activity - Cargo transport - Rural activity - Self-employed sales representatives - Other activities not characterised as providing services	8
- Transport services, except freight - Financial and similar institutions	16
- Services of: - Civil partnerships relating to a legally regulated profession - Business intermediation - Management, leasing or assignment of real estate, furniture and rights of any kind - Construction by administration or labour-only contract - Commercial representation on behalf of third parties - Factoring - Provision of any other kind of service	32

Source: Calculation of Real Profit in SPED (PEREIRA, 2009, p. 12)

The estimated percentages are applied to the gross revenue from activities that are part of the company's corporate objectives, as expressed in its articles of association. Gross revenue from sales and services includes the product of the sale of goods and services in own account operations, the price of services rendered and the result earned in third party account operations, noting that legal entities that carry out real estate activities relating to land subdivision, real estate development, construction of buildings intended for the sale of real estate built or acquired for resale should consider this as gross revenue. (PEREIRA, 2009, p.13)

Revenue should be included in the month in which each unit is completed; revenue from the supply of goods and services to a legal entity governed by public law or a company under its control, public companies, mixed-capital companies or their subsidiaries, in the case of contracted work or supply; revenue obtained by factoring companies, represented by the difference between the amount expressed in the credit security acquired and the amount paid, should be recognised on the date of the operation (PEREIRA, 2009, p.13).

They do not form part of the monthly income tax base:

- income and net gains from fixed and variable income financial investments;
- income and net gains produced by fixed and variable income financial investments that will be taken into account in determining the monthly income tax base when they have not been subject to the withholding tax or monthly payment provided for in the specific taxation rules to which they are subject;
- credit recoveries that do not represent new revenue;
- the reversal of the balance of previously constituted provisions;
- profits and dividends arising from shareholdings valued at acquisition cost and the offsetting adjustment for increases in the value of investments valued using the equity method;
- interest on own capital earned. The income tax rate in force for the calendar year is 15% (fifteen per cent) on the real profit calculated by legal entities in general, whether their object is commercial or civil (PEREIRA, 2009, p.15).

The portion of the real profit that exceeds the result of multiplying R$20,000.00 (twenty thousand reais) by the number of months in the respective calculation period is subject to the additional tax at a rate of 10% (ten per cent). Also subject to the surcharge is the portion of the estimated monthly tax base, in the case of legal entities that have opted for annual assessment of income tax, that exceeds R$20,000.00 (twenty thousand reais). The rate of the surcharge is the same for all legal entities, including financial institutions, insurance companies and the like (PEREIRA, 2009, p.15).The surcharge is also levied on the taxable results of legal entities that carry out rural activities. In the case of mixed activities, the basis for calculating the surcharge will be the sum of the real profit calculated in general activities and the real profit calculated in rural activities (PEREIRA, 2009, p.15).

4.7 Real Profit Calculation Book

The result for the current period must be adjusted by all the determined additions, exclusions and offsetting of tax losses allowed by income tax legislation. The statement of actual profit for the period covered by the suspension or reduction balance sheets or trial balances must be entered in the Actual Profit Calculation Book (Lalur). With each balance sheet or trial balance drawn up for the purpose of suspending or reducing tax, the taxpayer must determine a new real profit for the current period, disregarding those calculated in previous months of the same calendar year. The additions, exclusions and offsets of tax losses computed in the calculation of actual profit, corresponding to the balance sheets or trial balances, must be itemised in part A of Lalur, for the purposes of drawing up the statement of actual profit for the current period, with no entry being made in part B of said book (PEREIRA, 2009, p.11).

In the event of a tax loss, the legal entity will be exempt from paying the tax corresponding to the month in which the balance sheet or trial balance of suspension or reduction was drawn up. Legal entities subject to Real Profit may deduct the following tax incentives from the tax due:

- Cultural and artistic character.
- Workers' Food Programme.
- Industrial/Agricultural Technological Development, Audiovisual Activity.
- Children's and Adolescents' Rights Funds.
- Regional Tax Reduction and/or Exemption.
- Reduction for Reinvestment.

The tax incentives mentioned above, with the exception of those relating to Industrial/Agricultural Technological Development, Regional Tax Reductions and/or Exemptions, and Reinvestment Reductions, can be deducted from the tax due calculated on the monthly estimated tax base. The following can also be deducted: income tax paid or withheld at source on income that formed part of the basis for calculating the tax due; income tax paid abroad on profits made available, income and capital gains (PEREIRA, 2009, p.11).

e-LALUR

The Electronic Book of Bookkeeping and Calculation of Income Tax and Social Contribution on Net Income of Legal Entities Taxed by Real Profit (e-Lalur) was established by RFB Normative Instruction 989/2009. However, with the revocation of this Normative Instruction by IN RFB 1.353/2013, E-Lalur is now governed by the rules of the Tax Accounting Bookkeeping - ECF. In relation to events occurring as of 1st January 2014, legal entities are exempt from having to keep a physical book of the Real Profit Calculation Book (Lalur) and submit the Corporate Economic and Tax Information Statement (DIPJ). Therefore, it remains compulsory to keep the LALUR in digital form.

4.8 Social Contribution on Net Profit - CSLL

The CSLL rate is 9% (nine per cent) for taxable events occurring from 1° February 2000. For financial and similar institutions, the contribution rate has changed to 15 per cent and should only take effect in the second quarter of 2017. The rate will therefore be 9% until 30 April and 15% from 1° May 2017 (PEREIRA, 2009, p.19).

Legal entities taxed on a quarterly basis must calculate CSLL on a quarterly basis. The basis for calculating CSLL corresponds to net accounting profit adjusted by the additions determined, the exclusions allowed and the offsetting of negative calculation bases up to the limit defined in specific legislation in force at the time the taxable events occurred. The CSLL amount cannot be deducted for the purpose of determining actual profit. On the other hand, legal entities taxed under the annual real profit method must pay the CSLL monthly, determined on the estimated calculation base (PEREIRA, 2009, p.19).

The amounts of CSLL actually paid, calculated on the monthly estimated calculation basis, during the calendar year, may be deducted from the amount of CSLL calculated annually (adjustment). The amount of CSLL cannot be deducted for the purposes of determining actual profit or the calculation basis itself (Law no. 9.316/96, art. 1).°

In the case of activities carried out by legal entities of a commercial, industrial or service-providing nature, the CSLL base calculated on an estimated basis will be the sum of the following amounts: the amount corresponding to 12% (twelve per cent) of monthly gross revenue, excluding:

- Cancelled sales.
- Sales returns.
- Unconditional discounts granted.
- Non-cumulative taxes levied separately on the buyer, of which the seller of the goods or service provider is merely the depositary.
- Capital gains, other income.

Positive results arising from income not included in the activity, including:

- income earned on loan transactions between controlling, controlled, affiliated or interconnected legal entities;
- capital gains earned on the sale of permanent shareholdings in affiliated and controlled companies, and shareholdings that remained in the assets of the legal entity until the end of the calendar year following their acquisition;
- gains from *hedging* operations carried out on stock, commodities and futures exchanges or on the over-the-counter market;
- income from the rental of property, when this is not the corporate purpose of the legal entity, less the charges necessary to realise it;
- interest equivalent to the benchmark rate of the Special Settlement and Custody System (Selic), for federal securities, accumulated monthly, relating to taxes and contributions to be refunded or offset;
- active monetary variations; capital gains earned on the return of capital in goods and rights;
- the difference between the value in cash or the value of the goods and rights received from an exempt institution as a return of assets;
- the value in cash or the value of the goods and rights that have been handed over for the formation of said assets;
- income and net gains from fixed-income and variable-income financial investments (PEREIRA, 2009, p.17).

As of September 2003, under the provisions of Law 10.684/03, the percentage of profit for calculating the social contribution became *32%* for the following activities: provision of services in general; business intermediation; administration, leasing or assignment of real estate, furniture and rights of any nature; Factoring, (PEREIRA, 2009, p.18).

The same form of taxation adopted by the legal entity for the purposes of calculating income tax must be adopted for the purposes of calculating CSLL. Thus, the legal entity that drew up a balance sheet or trial balance to suspend or reduce the payment of income tax in a given month of the calendar year must calculate the CSLL calculation base on the net profit calculated in that same balance sheet, adjusted by the additions determined, the exclusions allowed and the compensations for the negative CSLL calculation base, observing the limits defined in the relevant legislation, even if the calculated calculation base is higher than the value of the estimated calculation base (PEREIRA, 2009, p.19).

The legal entity that draws up a balance sheet or trial balance suspending or reducing the payment of IRPJ and CSLL on 31 December must include profits from abroad made available under the terms of art. 1° of Law No. 9,532/97. The legal entity must also include income and capital gains earned abroad in this balance sheet for the purposes of the CSLL (PEREIRA, 2009, p.19).

The legal entity may offset the negative calculation basis, provided it keeps the books and documents required by tax legislation to prove the amount of this basis used for offsetting.

The negative tax base of activities in general can be offset against the positive tax base of rural activities calculated in the same calculation period, or vice versa. The negative tax base of activities in general and rural activities, calculated as of the end of the 1995 calendar year, may be offset, cumulatively with the negative tax base calculated up to 31 December 1994, against the result of the calculation period adjusted by the additions and exclusions provided for in the legislation, determined in subsequent calendar years, subject to the maximum reduction limit of thirty per cent, in the case of the negative tax base of activities in general. (PEREIRA, 2009, p.19)

The legal entity may not offset its own negative tax base if, between the date of calculation and the date of offsetting, there has been a cumulative change in its corporate control and branch of activity. The legal entity that succeeds by incorporation, merger or spin-off cannot offset the negative tax base of the successor. In the case of a partial demerger, the demerged legal entity may offset its own negative tax base, in proportion to the remaining portion of its net assets. (PEREIRA, 2009, p.19)The CSLL determined monthly on the basis of gross revenue and accruals or on a balance sheet or trial balance of suspension or reduction shall be paid by the last working day of the month following that to which the calculation refers. The legal entity may offset the tax loss calculated in the statement of actual profit and recorded in the Actual Profit Calculation Book (Lalur), provided it keeps the books and documents required by tax legislation to prove the amount of the tax loss used for offsetting (PEREIRA, 2009, p.19).

4.9 Real Profit Calculation

At the end of each quarter, year or current balance sheet/balance sheet period in order to suspend/reduce the monthly payment of IRPJ/CSLL, the legal entity must calculate the calculation basis on which Income Tax will be levied (PEREIRA, 2009, p.22).

As the net profit calculated in the accounts does not normally correspond to the profit to be taxed, the legal entity must determine the real profit, on which it will calculate the IRPJ due, including the additional tax when applicable. The calculation basis on which income tax should be levied is determined using the Real Profit Calculation Book (Lalur).

The purpose of this book is to show the adjustments to the result of the IRPJ calculation period, through the prescribed or authorised additions, exclusions or compensations, which will serve as elements for completing the Statement of Actual Profit (DIPJ) (PEREIRA, 2009, p.22).

Lalur is a fundamental part of the calculation of real profit. Therefore, all legal entities subject to this form of taxation are obliged to record it, even if by choice. To determine the real profit, they must be added to the net profit for the calculation period:

- costs, expenses, charges, losses, provisions, participations and any amounts deducted in the calculation of actual net profit which, according to tax legislation, are not considered deductible;
- results, income, revenues and any other amounts not included in the calculation of net profit which, according to tax legislation, must be computed in the determination of actual profit (PEREIRA, 2009, p.22).

The following must be excluded from net profit in each calculation period: amounts whose deduction is authorised by tax legislation and which have not been computed in the calculation of net profit; results, income, revenue and any other amounts included in the calculation of net profit which, according to tax legislation, should not be computed in real profit, considered as non-taxable amounts. Tax losses calculated in previous periods can be offset against real profit (PEREIRA, 2009, p.22).

4.10 Provisions

These are amounts arising from expenses incurred, known or calculable. The provision for doubtful debtors or provision for doubtful accounts is intended to recognise a probable loss in the Asset accounts, which represent the rights receivable (Duplicates receivable, Customers, Promissory Notes receivable, etc.) (CÂNDIDO, 2008, p.81).

There are two aspects to this provision: the so-called technical provision and the tax provision. In the technical provision, a percentage is calculated on the value of the rights receivable, and the result is added to the cost and/or expense for the year. This type of provision complies with accounting principles, such as the principle of prudence, bookkeeping rules and commercial legislation (CÂNDIDO, 2008, p.81).

From a tax perspective, the provision for doubtful accounts is considered to have an impact on the company's results, because it reduces profit or increases losses. The Internal Revenue Service issued Law 9430 in 1996, which limits the amounts that companies can recognise as costs or expenses. The management percentage that companies apply can be measured using statistical techniques. However, the IRS has established fixed amounts to be considered in the provision (CÂNDIDO, 2008, p.81).

Legal entities taxed on actual profit (quarterly or annually), including companies that draw up a balance sheet or trial balance during the year for the purposes of suspending or reducing monthly income tax by estimate, may record losses on the receipt of credits arising from their activities as deductible expenses, provided that the requirements laid down in Law No. 9.430/96 and IN SRF No. 93/97 are complied with (CÂNDIDO, 2008, p.81).

4.10.1 Rules for recording credit losses

Below are the rules for recording credit losses. These losses refer to customers who have been declared insolvent, who have unsecured securities or who have provided collateral, but whose securities are overdue within the limits set by law, and the rules governing them are as follows:

I - In relation to which the debtor has been declared insolvent in a judgement issued by the Judiciary.

II - Without a value guarantee: up to R$5,000.00 (five thousand reais) per operation, overdue for more than six months, regardless of whether legal proceedings have already been initiated to collect it; above R$5,000.00 (five thousand reais) up to R$30.000.00 (thirty thousand reais), per operation, overdue for more than one year, regardless of whether legal proceedings have already been initiated to collect them, but administrative collection is maintained; over R$30,000.00 (thirty thousand reais), overdue for more than one year, provided that legal proceedings to collect them have been initiated and maintained.

III - Guaranteed: overdue for more than two years, provided that the legal proceedings for their collection have been initiated and maintained. Guaranteed credit is considered to come from sales with reservation of ownership, fiduciary alienation in guarantee or operations with other real guarantees. A transaction is considered to be the sale of goods, the provision of services, the assignment of rights, the investment of financial resources in transactions with securities contained in a single contract, which provides for the form of payment of the agreed price, even if the transaction is carried out for payment in more than one instalment. In the case of mercantile companies, the transaction will be characterised by the issue of the invoice, even if it includes more than one invoice.

For the purposes of recording the loss, credits will be considered at their original value plus adjustment, interest and any other late payment charges. In the case of a credit agreement in which the non-payment of one or more instalments implies the automatic maturity of all other outstanding instalments, they will be considered in relation to the total credits, per operation, with the same debtor (Law No. 9.430/96 and IN SRF No. 93/97).

4.10.2 Deductible provisions

According to Neves and Viceconti (2007, p.228), for triggering events occurring after 01/01/1997, they are only deductible:

- Provision for holidays.
- Provision for thirteenth salary.
- Technical provisions of insurance companies, capitalisation companies and private pension entities, whose constitution is required by the special legislation applicable to them.

For taxable events occurring from 1 January 2002 onwards, the amount of technical provisions for health care plan operations, the constitution of which is required by special legislation applicable to them, may be deducted. Companies that carry out the following activities related to the publishing, distribution and retail sale of books may also set aside a provision for inventory losses (deductible when calculating the IRPJ and CSLL tax base), calculated on the last day of each tax calculation period, corresponding to 1/3 of the value of the inventory existing on that date. (NEVES e VICECONTI, 2007, p.228)

SRF Normative Instruction no. 412 of 23/03/2004, in its article 4° , established that the accounting records pertinent to the provision for loss of inventories should be as follows:

- the provision will be debited from the profit and loss account and credited to the inventory reduction account;
- the provision will be reversed by debiting the inventory reduction account and crediting the profit and loss account;
- the actual loss will be debited from the inventory reduction account, until its value and the excess, debited from the profit and loss account (costs or expenses) and credited to the inventory account;
- the recovery of losses that have affected taxable income, debiting the equity account and crediting the profit and loss account (NEVES and VICECONTI, 2007, p.229).

Indeductible provisions are set up to comply with accounting principles or for other reasons. If they are non-deductible, they must be added to net income in the calculation period, under "A" of Lalur for the purposes of determining taxable income. These are: provision for bonuses to directors, provision for tax risks or contingencies, provision for contingencies, provision for redemption of beneficiary shares. The amount of the provision must be controlled in part B of the LALUR, since if it is reversed, the corresponding income will not be taxed (NEVES and VICECONTI, 2007, p.229).

4.10.3 Reversal of Provisions

According to Neves and Viceconti (2007, p.235), if the expense incurred in setting up the provision cannot be deducted when determining the real profit, the income resulting from its eventual reversal in subsequent assessment periods will not be taxed by the tax authorities, so that there is no double incidence of tax. To this end, the legal entity must control the amount of the provision, which has been added to net income, in part "B" of Lalur. In the calculation period in which the provision is reversed, the company must exclude the respective amount from net income, writing it off in part "B" of Lalur. The reversal of this provision will constitute income that should be classified as operating in the Income Statement for the year in the group other operating income (NEVES and VICECONTI, 2007, p.235).

The write-off of bad debts must comply with the criteria established by tax legislation in order to be deductible in determining taxable income. For the sake of simplicity, it is therefore recommended that the Allowance for Doubtful Accounts be reversed in full in the following accounting period and that the legal entity write off bad debts in accordance with the criteria of its own legislation. If the company intends to write off bad debts according to its own criteria and/or by debiting the allowance account, if there is a difference in relation to the amount obtained according to tax criteria, this should be recorded in part "A" of Lalur. For subsequent quarters, the calculation will be made by applying the 15% rate to the CSLL calculation base, calculated in accordance with tax legislation. In the case of annual calculation, the percentage ratio between the total gross revenue for the months of May to the last month covered by the calculation period (the general rule is December) and the total gross revenue computed in the balance sheet for that period is used (NEVES and VICECONTI, 2007, p.235).

4.11 Real Profit Income Tax Deductions

Legal entities subject to Real Profit may deduct the following tax incentives from the tax due:

4.11.1 Cultural and artistic character

The legal entity can deduct from the tax due the amounts actually made in the calculation period as donations or sponsorship, both through contributions to the National Culture Fund (FNC) in the form of donations, under the terms of Law no. 8.313/91, and through direct support for projects: cultural projects approved under the terms of the regulations of the National Cultural Support Programme (Pronac); related to cultural production, in the following segments:

- performing arts;
- books of artistic, literary or humanistic value;
- classical or instrumental music;
- visual arts exhibitions;
- donations of collections to public libraries, museums, public archives and film libraries;

  - training staff and acquiring equipment to maintain these collections;
  - production of short and medium-length cinematographic and videophonographic works;
  - preservation and dissemination of the audiovisual collection;
  - preservation of tangible and intangible cultural heritage;
  - relating to the production of independently produced Brazilian cinematographic and videophonographic works;
  - co-production of independently produced Brazilian cinematographic and videophonographic works, telefilms, miniseries, documentaries, fiction, animations and independently produced Brazilian educational and cultural television programmes, approved by the National Film Agency (Ancine), provided that they are produced with the resources referred to in item X of the same art. 39.

Cultural projects must be previously approved by the Ministry of Culture (MinC), subject to the provisions of its acts issued for this purpose. The projects referred to in letters a and b, related to cinematographic and videophonographic works, must be previously approved by the MinC or Ancine. The legal entity may deduct the calculated amount of this incentive from the tax due, observing the legislation granting the projects and the legal limits established, as follows:

- Projects approved under the terms of articles 25 and 26 of Law No. 8.313/91: 40% of the sum of donations; 30% of the sum of sponsorships;
- Projects approved under the terms of art. 18 of Law no. 8.313/91: 100% of the sum of donations or sponsorships.

Donations made in favour of the FNC can be deducted, as long as they are proven by a bank deposit receipt and a declaration of receipt signed by the donor. The deduction of income tax under this heading alone may not exceed 4 per cent of the income tax due.

In addition to observing the specific limit for each incentive, the total deductions relating to incentives in cultural operations and audiovisual activity, including those relating to investments in the National Film Industry Financing Funds (Funcines) cannot exceed 4% of the tax due (PEREIRA, 2009, p. 26).

4.11.2 - Workers' Food Programme - PAT

Legal entities that have Worker's Meal Programmes approved by the Ministry of Labour, respecting the limit established in the legislation, can deduct from income tax the amount equivalent to 15% of the total costing expenses incurred in the calculation period. To use the benefit, the maximum cost of the meal is R$2.49 (two reais and forty-nine cents), if the actual cost is higher than this amount.

The monthly value of the benefit is calculated by applying the tax rate to the result of multiplying the number of meals provided in each calculation period, corresponding to 80% of the effective cost of each meal. If the effective cost is equal to or greater than R$2.49, the monthly value of the benefit is calculated by applying the tax rate to the result of multiplying the number of meals provided in the calculation period by the value of R$1.99 (one real and ninety-nine cents). The legal entity that is calculating annual real profit must consider the value of the benefit to be the result of the sum of the values corresponding to the months of the calendar year, observing the limits in relation to the tax due (PEREIRA, 2009, p. 26).

This deduction alone cannot exceed 4 per cent of the income tax due. Any excess can be carried over for deduction in the following two calendar years. Subject to the specific limit for each incentive, the total tax deductions, calculated at the end of the quarterly or annual period (adjustment), or in the period corresponding to the balance sheet or trial balance of suspension or reduction, relating to the PAT - Workers' Food Programme and the Industrial Technological Development Programmes (PDTI) and the Agricultural Technological Development Programme (PDTA), cannot exceed 4% of the tax due (PEREIRA, 2009, p. 26).

Table III below shows the amounts relating to the implementation of the Workers' Food Programme implemented by **SILAS SANCHES S.A. in** 2017.

TABLE III

Workers' Food Programme - PAT **SILAS SANCHES S/A** in 2017

	1° Quarter	2° Quarter	3° Quarter	4° Quarter
Acquisition value	181.275,74	256.739,40	239.649,80	233.983,59
Recovered value	(523,90)	(1.146,60)	(1.352,72)	(1.025,26)
Total value of expenditure	180.751,84	255.592,80	238.297,08	232.958,33

Source: Profit and Loss Account of Silas Sanches S/A as at 31/03/2017

To calculate the annual PAT, the total purchase price minus the amount recovered was divided by the unit value of R$13.95 (the value of the daily unit meal voucher provided to each employee) to find out the number of meal vouchers, and then the amount found was multiplied by R$1.99, which is the maximum cost of the meal accepted by income tax legislation to arrive at the calculation base before applying the 15% incentive rate.Table IV below illustrates the calculation of the Workers' Food

Programme incentive, used as a reduction in IRPJ.

TABLE IV

180,751.84 + 255,592.80 + 238,237.08 + 232,958.33 = 907,540.02 /13.95 = 65,056 x 1.99 = 129,461.44 x 15% = 19,419.22. R$ 19,419.22 is the amount of the annual incentive that has been deducted from the amount of tax payable. to be paid by Cia Silas Sanches S/A as Corporate Income Tax.

Workers' Food Programme-PAT **SILAS SANCHES S/A** 2017

Source: Profit and Loss Account of Silas Sanches S/A as at 31/03/2017

4.11. 3Audiovisual Activity

Legal entities subject to the real profit tax can deduct from the tax due the amounts related to investments in projects: of independent production of Brazilian cinematographic audiovisual works; specific to the audiovisual, cinematographic area of exhibition, distribution and technical infrastructure presented by a Brazilian company; of production of Brazilian cinematographic and videophonographic works of feature, medium and short films of independent production, of co-production of Brazilian cinematographic and videophonographic works of independent production, of telefilms, miniseries, documentaries, fictional films, animations and television programmes of an educational and cultural nature, Brazilian of independent production.

Projects must be previously approved by Ancine. Subject to the specific limit for each incentive, the total tax deductions for the Audiovisual Activity and Cultural Activity incentives may not exceed 4 per cent of the tax (PEREIRA, 2009, p. 27).

In monthly estimated tax payments, the portion of the incentive in excess of the individual limit, verified in each month, can be deducted in subsequent months, until December of the same year or when calculating the tax due in the annual adjustment; the amount in excess of the limit calculated in the annual adjustment cannot be deducted from the tax due in subsequent periods. If the amount of the incentive deducted in the monthly payments by estimate is higher than that calculated on the basis of the tax due in the annual adjustment, the difference must be paid within the same period set for the payment of the single income tax instalment, in compliance with the relevant tax legislation (PEREIRA, 2009, p. 27).

In order to calculate the donation amounts for Cia Silas Sanches S/A's Audiovisual Activity and Cultural Activity in 2017, the amount of the quarterly Corporate Income Tax calculation was added and a 4% rate was applied.

Table V below illustrates the calculation of the incentive for Cia Silas Sanches S/A's audiovisual and cultural activities in 2017.

TABLE V

Audiovisual and Cultural Activity of **SILAS SANCHES S.A.** in 2017

186.522,02 + 178.761,45 + 133.408,77 + 192.176,74 x 4% = 27.634,76

Amount of Cia Silas Sanches S/A's Audiovisual and Cultural Activity incentive in 2017 that could have been deducted from Corporate Income Tax (IRPJ)

Source: Silas Sanches Profit and Loss Account as at 31/03/2017

The amount of R$27,634.76 could have been deducted from the amount paid in income tax if Cia Silas Sanches S/A had sponsored audiovisual or cultural activities in 2017.

4.11.4Funds for the Rights of Children and Adolescents

Legal entities can deduct from the income tax due for each assessment period the total of donations made to the national, state or municipal Funds for the Rights of Children and Adolescents, duly substantiated. The maximum deduction allowed is 1 per cent of the tax due. The tax deduction for donations made to the Funds for the Rights of Children and Adolescents is not subject to an overall limit. The amount corresponding to the donations made is not deductible as an operating expense in determining the real profit and the basis for calculating the social contribution on net profit (PEREIRA, 2009, p. 28).Chart VI, presented below, illustrates the calculation of the incentive relating to the fund for the rights of children and adolescents at Cia Silas Sanches S/A in 2017.

TABLE VI

SILAS SANCHES S.A. Child and Adolescent Rights Funds in 2017

	1° Quarter	2° Quarter	3° Quarter	4° Quarter
Amount of donation to the FIA	1.000,00	1.000,00	1.000,00	1.000,00

Source: Profit and Loss Account of Silas Sanches S/A as at 31/03/2017

In 2017, Cia Silas Sanches S/A donated a total of R$ 4,000.00 (four thousand reais) to the Fund for the Rights of Children and Adolescents. Table VII below shows how much Cia Silas Sanches S/A could have donated to the Fund for the Rights of Children and Adolescents, as the amount donated was well below the permitted limit.

TABLE VII

Audiovisual and Cultural Activity of **SILAS SANCHES S.A.** in 2017

186.522,02 + 178.761,45 + 133.408,77 + 192.176,74 x 1% = 19.217,67 Amount of the incentive to the Fund for the Rights of Children and Adolescents of Cia Silas Saches S/A in 2017 that could have been deducted from Corporate Income Tax (IRPJ)

Source: Profit and Loss Account of Silas Sanches S/A as at 31/03/2017

In 2017, Cia Silas Sanches S/A could have donated a total of R$ 19,217.67 (nineteen thousand two hundred and seventeen reais and sixty-seven centavos) to the Fund for the Rights of Children and Adolescents.

4.11. 5Industrial/Agricultural Technological Development PDTI/PDTA

The legal entity that holds an Industrial Technological Development Programme (PDTI) or Agricultural Technological Development Programme (PDTA), under the terms of Decree 96.760/88, can deduct from the tax due the amount equivalent to the result of applying the 15% rate to the total expenditure made on technological development activities in the calculation period, subject to the limits allowed (PEREIRA, 2009, p. 28).

The income tax deduction under this heading alone cannot exceed 4% of the income tax due. Subject to the specific limit for each incentive, the total deductions from tax due for the PAT - Workers' Food Programme and the Industrial Technological Development Programmes (PDTI) and Agricultural Technological Development Programme (PDTA) may not exceed 4% of the tax due. For projects approved before 03/06/1993, the

The individual deduction limit is 8 per cent (PEREIRA, 2009, p. 28).

The PDTI/PDTA incentives, whose projects were approved after 3 June 1993, cannot be used cumulatively with others of the same nature provided for in a previous or subsequent law (PEREIRA, 2009, p. 28).

4.11.6 Sports or para-sports activity

From the 2007 calendar year until the 2015 calendar year, inclusive, the amounts spent as sponsorship or donations in direct support of sports and para-sports projects previously approved by the Ministry of Sport may be deducted from the income tax due, calculated in each quarterly or annual calculation period, by the legal entity taxed on the basis of real profit (PEREIRA, 2009, p. 28).

Deductions are limited to one per cent of the tax due for each calculation period. Legal entities will not be able to deduct the amounts incentivised for the purposes of determining actual profit and the basis for calculating the Social Contribution on Net Profit (CSLL). The benefits of this item do not exclude or reduce other tax benefits and deductions in force (PEREIRA, 2009, p. 28).

Amounts earmarked for sponsorship or donations in favour of projects that directly or indirectly benefit individuals or legal entities linked to the donor or sponsor are not deductible. The following are considered to be linked to the sponsor or donor: the legal entity of which the sponsor or donor is the owner, administrator, manager, shareholder or partner, on the date of the operation or in the previous twelve months; the spouse, relatives up to the third degree, including those related, and dependents of the sponsor, donor or owners, administrators, shareholders or partners of the legal entity linked to the sponsor or donor, under the terms of item I of this paragraph; and a related, controlling or controlled legal entity, or one whose owners, directors, shareholders or partners are any of the persons referred to in item II of this paragraph (PEREIRA, 2009, p. 28). 28).

Table VIII below shows how much Cia Silas Sanches S/A could have encouraged sports or para-sports activities.

TABLE VIII

SILAS SANCHES S.A. Sporting or Para-sporting Activity in 2017

186.522,02 + 178.761,45 + 133.408,77 + 192.176,74 x 1% = 19.217,67 Amount of the incentive for Sports or Para-sports Activities of Cia Silas Sanches S/A in 2017 that could have been deducted from Corporate Income Tax (IRPJ)

Source: Profit and Loss Account of Silas Sanches S/A as at 31/03/2017

4.12 Return on Equity

For taxable events occurring from 01/01/1996 onwards, legal entities may deduct interest paid or credited individually to owners, partners or shareholders, as remuneration on equity, calculated on the net assets account and limited to the pro rata day variation of the Long Term Interest Rate (TJLP), for the purposes of calculating the real profit, observing the accrual basis. The amount of interest paid or credited, for the purposes of deductibility as a financial expense, may not exceed fifty per cent of the greater of the net profit corresponding to the calculation period (quarterly or annual) in which the interest was paid or credited, after deduction of CSLL and before provision for income tax and deduction of said interest; or the balances of retained earnings and profit reserves from previous periods. The amount of interest on own capital is considered to be credited individually when the expense is recorded in the legal entity's bookkeeping, against an account or sub-account of its payable liabilities, representing the credit right of the partner or shareholder of the company or the owner of a sole proprietorship (NEVES and VICECONTI, 2007, p. 266).

The headline of Consultation Solution No. 63/01 of the 6ª Tax Region - Deduction of Interest from Previous Periods states that a legal entity is prohibited from calculating the amount of interest on equity from previous periods in one financial year, under penalty of violating the accrual basis of accounting. ªFor the purposes of calculating interest on own capital, the profit for the calculation period itself must not be included as part of net assets (the subject of Consultation Solution No. 95/00 of the 10th Tax Region); interest paid or credited must not be included as part of net assets.

individually to the owner, partners, shareholders, in the manner advocated by article 9º of Law 9,249/95, as remuneration for equity capital that has not been computed in the calculation of equity capital that has not been computed in the calculation of net profit for the year, may be excluded for the purposes of determining actual profit (Consultation Decision No. 068/98, of the 7ª RF).

The deductibility of interest on own capital extends to the basis for calculating the Social Contribution on Net Profit (CSLL) for triggering events occurring as of 1st January 1997. The amount of interest paid or credited by the legal entity, as remuneration of equity, may be imputed to the amount of dividends, without prejudice to its deductibility in the real profit and in the CSLL calculation base, as long as the payment of Income Tax at Source is made. The amount of interest paid or credited as return on equity will be subject to income tax at source at the rate of 15% on the date of payment or credit (NEVES e VICECONTI, 2007, p. 266).Table IX below illustrates the calculation of interest on equity at Cia Silas Sanches S/A in 2017.

TABLE IX

Interest on Equity

Net Worth of Cia Silas Sanches S/A on 31/12/2007
The amount of interest paid or credited, for the purpose of deductibility as a financial expense, may not exceed 50 per cent of Profit Before Income Tax after Social Contribution on Net Profit for 2017, nor exceed 50 per cent of the Profit Reserve plus Retained Earnings for 2016.
CSLL .... (419,102.00) Profit .... 3,497,757.00x 50% = 1,748,878.50 Retained Earnings and Profit Reserves for 2016 Legal Reserve 237,475.00 Profit reserve for expansion .... 1,173,409.00 Total ....1,410,884.00 x 50% = 705,442.00
Note: The amount of interest did not exceed 50 per cent of the 2017 result, but it did exceed 50 per cent of the profit reserves. In this case, the amount to be paid in interest will be: 705,442.00.

Source: Silas Sanches Profit and Loss Account as at 31/03/2017

CHAPTER 5

TAX PLANNING AT SILAS SANCHES S/A FOR THE 2017 FINANCIAL YEAR

5.1 Practice: Tax Planning Simulation

To simulate the information, in order to find the best option for the tax regime that would result in a lower tax burden, tax planning, the accounting statements calculated in 2017 were collected, such as the Trial Balance, Balance Sheet, Quarterly Income Statement - Real Profit Calculation Book, all attached.

The Trial Balance showed the balance of all the accounts needed to prepare the Income Statement for the Year - DRE, which are revenues, costs and expenses. This statement was calculated on a quarterly basis, since **CIAS SILAS SANCHES S/A** chose the Real Profit Quarterly taxation system for 2017.

After a survey of all the asset accounts in the Trial Balance, the Accounting Department identified, among the profit and loss accounts, those that would result in tax savings, in accordance with differentiated legal treatment. These are

- Provision for Doubtful Debts;
- Interest on Equity;
- Income tax deductions.

Taxes were calculated quarterly in the Income Statement.

After selecting the statements used to calculate the PIS, COFINS, IRPJ and CSLL taxes for 2017, the Income Statement was prepared using the legal forms of tax savings applicable to the structure of **CIA SILAS SANCHES S.A.**

The practical model carried out proved that if **CIA SILAS SANCHES S.A** had adopted Tax Planning at the beginning of 2017, it would have had a reduction in

its tax burden in the amount of R$ 319,555.75.

The practical model also proved that **CIA SILAS SANCHES S.A.** made the correct choice of tax regime, Real Profit, among the options available in Brazil and within the limits stipulated by the Income Tax legislation.

According to the Income Tax Law, **CIA SILAS SANCHES S.A.** has the option of choosing its form of taxation as Real Profit or Presumed Profit, since it does not qualify as Simples Nacional.

The practical model, when simulating the amount of taxes that would be paid under the Presumed Profit regime, found the amount to be R$3,646,281.11. In this type of tax regime, taxes are determined on the basis of gross revenue, using variable rates. In the case of **CIA SILAS SANCHES S.A.,** this rate is the highest, 32%, due to the line of business in which the company operates, the provision of services. Presumed profit is a presumption on the part of the tax authorities of what a company's profit would be if accounting didn't exist.

The calculation of the taxes to be paid for the Tax Planning simulation was carried out within the legal criteria, taking into account both the rules and the principles that govern Accounting

Science.

In addition to Real Profit income tax deductions, such as the Workers' Food Programme (PAT), cultural and artistic incentives, industrial technological development, farming and audiovisual activities and the Children's and Adolescents' Rights Fund.

Losses were also recognised in provisions for doubtful debtors on overdue securities, in accordance with the Income Tax Regulations.

The most significant tax saving is due to the change in the return on equity. Instead of the shareholders being paid dividends, they would be paid interest on equity. In this case, the payment of interest on equity is used as a deductible expense, making the profit and taxes levied on it lower.

It is important to emphasise that the shareholders' remuneration would also be higher with interest on equity. In 2017, the shareholders received R$537,561.00 in dividends, while they would have received R$705,442.00 in interest on equity, less 15% withholding tax of R$105,816.30, giving a net amount of R$599,625.70.

It can be seen that the shareholders were penalised R$62,064.70 in the distribution of **CIA SILAS SANCHES S.A.'s** profit in 2017. Tax planning not only benefits the company by reducing its tax burden, but it can also provide a better distribution of profits to the company's biggest stakeholders, the shareholders. Table X below illustrates the net profit for 2017 in the Income Statement of **CIA SILAS SANCHES S.A.**

TABLE X:
CIA SILAS SANCHES S.A
ANNUAL INCOME STATEMENT 2017

GROSS OPERATING REVENUE	**23.981.730,99**
Services	23.981.730,99
DEDUCTION FROM GROSS REVENUE	**-1.733.608,09**
Tax invoiced	-1.659.236,77
Cancelled Services	-74.371,32
NET OPERATING REVENUE	**22.248.122,90**
Gross Profit	**22.248.122,90**
OPERATING EXPENSES	**-19.082.076,16**
Staff	-7.842.717,91
Charges, Social	-2.773.721,52
Other Income	-2.204.359,66
Consumables	-1.483.652,40
Services and Insurance	-21.113.022,36
Taxes	-138.615,33
Depreciation	-953.416,21
Other Operating Expenses	-1.267.165,77
Interest on Equity	-705.442,00
Sub total	**-38.482.113,16**
Reversal of Expenses	10.076.839,00
DRC recovery	8.090.278,00
Financial Income	1.232.920,00
Sub total	**19.400.037,00**
OPERATING PROFIT	**3.166.046,74**
OTHER INCOME	182.642,31
OTHER EXPENSES	-137.272,03

	45.370,28
ACCOUNTING PROFIT BEFORE 1. INCOME AND CONT. SOCIAL	**3.211.417,02**
(-) Social Contribution	**-355.612,13**
(-) Income tax	**-843.891,12**
ANNUAL ACCOUNTING PROFIT 2017	**2.011.913,77**

Source: DRE of Silas Sanches 2017

Table XI below illustrates the sum of the taxes paid by Cia Silas Sanches S/A in 2017 without the use of tax planning.

TABLE XI

Real Profit Tax Calculation without Tax Planning

PIS	R$370.343,19
COFINS	R$1,363,264.81
IRPJ	R$1.099.957,00
CSLL	R$419.102,00
Total taxes paid in 2017	R$3,252,667.00

Source: Annual Income Statement of Cia Silas Sanches S/A

Table XII below illustrates the sum of Cia Silas Sanches S/A's taxes in 2017 using tax planning.

TABLE XII

Real Profit Tax Calculation with Tax Planning

PIS	R$370.343,19
COFINS	R$1,363,264.81
IRPJ	R$843.891,12
CSLL	R$355.612,13
Total taxes to be paid in 2017	R$2,933,111.25

Source: Annual Income Statement of Cia Silas Sanches S/A

Table XIII below illustrates the sum of Cia Silas Sanches S/A's taxes in 2017 calculated using Presumed Profit.

TABLE XIII

Calculation of Taxes by Presumed Profit

Gross Revenue from Services	R$23,981,730.99
Net Financial Income	R$1,232,920.00
Capital gain	R$45,370.28
Calculation Base	R$25,260,021.37
PIS	R$164.190,14
COFINS	R$757.800,64

(the rates applied were: PIS: 0.65% and COFINS: 3.00%)
IRPJ Total .... RevenuesR$25 ,260,021.37
Rate for calculation base 32%. Calculation BaseR$ 8,083,206.84
Tax rate 15%. .... IRPJR$1 .212.481,03
IRPJ ADDITIONAL Total RevenuesR$ 25.260.021,37
Rate for calculation base 32%. Calculation BaseR$ 8,083,206.84
Deduction for Calculation Base (240,000.00) .... (R$ 240,000.00)
Calculation BasisR$ 7,843,206.84
Tax rate 10%. ADDITIONALR$ 784,320.68
CSLL Total .... RevenuesR$25 ,260,021.37
Rate for calculation base 32%. Calculation BaseR$ 3,031,202.56
Tax rate 9%. .... CSLLR$727 .488,62
Total taxes to be paid in .... 2017R$3 ,646,281.11

Source: Annual Income Statement of Cia Silas Sanches S/A

Table XIV below illustrates the total taxes for 2017 calculated by the tax regimes that Cia Silas Sanches S/A falls under.

TABLE XIV

Comparison of total taxes calculated by the Real Profit without Tax Planning, Real Profit with Tax Planning and Presumed Profit regimes

Presumed ProfitR$ 3,646,281.11
Real Profit without Tax PlanningR$ 3,252,667.00
Real Profit with Tax .... PlanningR$2 ,933,111.25
Tax .... SavingsR$319 ,555.75

Source: Annual Income Statement of Cia Silas Sanches S/A

CHAPTER 6

FINAL CONSIDERATIONS

Tax planning is practised by many companies and denotes the business community's concern with organising its activities in the most productive way.

From what has been shown above, it is possible for companies to reduce their tax burden within the tax rules in force, either by taking advantage of incentives, deductions and exemptions, or even by making different tax options to those that are actually adopted, but always putting Tax Planning at the forefront, i.e. decisions must be made after simulations that indicate the best way to achieve the lowest tax burden. In the chapter on the National Tax System, the types of taxes by sphere were analysed, as well as the taxable event and the person liable to pay them.

Chapter 3, Tax Planning, discusses the importance and necessity of tax planning and the concepts of tax evasion and tax avoidance. Chapter 4 was dedicated to the study of tax regimes, with emphasis on Real Profit. The practical model carried out in Chapter 5 showed a reduction in the tax burden of R$ 290,772.34 if tax planning were implemented at the beginning of 2017.

Despite this, however, for the sake of survival in the competitive market, executives must have an administrative-financial vision of their businesses. Planning is no longer an option, but a necessity.

REFERENCES

AMARO, Luciano. *Brazilian Tax Law.* São Paulo: Saraiva 1997.

ARAÚJO, A.J.B. *Tax avoidance as an economic phenomenon and its legal consequences.* Jus Navigandi, Teresina, year 6, n. 59, October 2002. Available at: <http://jus2.uol.com.br/doutrina/texto.asp?id=3285>. Accessed on: 10 Dec 2007.

AMARAL, Gilberto Luiz do. *A nova ótica do Planejamento Tributário Empresarial.* Curitiba: IBPT, 2009.

BRAGA, F.G. *Elisão fiscal: a inconstitucionalidade da desconsideração de negócios jurídicos lícitos.* Jus Navigandi, Teresina, year 8, n. 359, July 2004. Available at: <http://jus2.uol.com.br/doutrina/texto.asp?id=5369>. Accessed on: 15 Dec 2009.

BALEEIRO Aliomar. *Uma Introdução à Ciência das Finanças.* 12. ed. Rio de Janeiro: Forense, 1977.

BALEEIRO Aliomar. *An Introduction to the Science of Finance.* 13 ed. Rio de Janeiro: Forense, 2001.

BECKER, Alfredo Augusto. *General Theory of Tax Law.* São Paulo: Saraiva, 1972.

BRAZIL. Constitution (1988). Constitution of the Federative Republic of Brazil: promulgated on 5 October 1988, updated up to Constitutional Amendment no. 23 of 1999 and by Constitutional Revision Amendments no. 1 to 6 of 1994. 12. Brasília: Federal Chamber.

BRAZIL. Constitution (1988). Complementary Law 155/2016

BRAZIL. Law no. 5. 172, of 25 October 1966. Called the NATIONAL TAX CODE by art. 7° . of Complementary Act no. 36, of 13 March 1967. Provides for the National Tax System and Establishes General Tax Law Rules Applicable to the Union, States and Municipalities. Amended by Complementary Law no. 118, of 9 February 2005. Federal Official Gazette. Brasília, 25 Oct 1966.

BORGES, Humberto Bonavides. *Tax Planning.* 5. ed. São Paulo: Atlas, 1996.

BORGES, Humberto Bonavides. *Tax Planning.* 6. ed. São Paulo: Atlas, 2001.

CAMPOS, Dejalma de. *Tax Law,* São Paulo: IPD IOB, 1991.

CAMPOS, Dejalma de. *Tax Procedural Practice.* São Paulo: Cultura Jurídica, 1996.

CÂNDIDO, Marlúcio. *General Accounting.* Belo Horizonte: FEAD, 2008

CAMPOS, Cândido H. *Prática de Planejamento Tributário - How to do Tax Planning* São Paulo: Quartier Latin, 2007.

CARRAZZA, R.A. *Curso de Direito Constitucional Tributário.* 17. ed. São Paulo: Malheiros Editores, 2002.

CARVALHO, P.B. Curso de Direito Tributário. 13. ed. São Paulo: Saraiva, 2000.

DOMINGUES, Nereu Miguel Ribeiro. The Effects of Tax Planning on Accounting. In: BRAZILIAN ACCOUNTING CONGRESS, XVI, 2000, Goiânia: Federal Accounting Council, Theme 8: Accounting and taxation.

DÓRIA, Antônio Roberto Sampaio. *Evasion and Elision.* 1. ed. São Paulo: Bushatsky, 1971.

DÓRIA, Antônio Roberto Sampaio. *Evasion and Elision. 2.* ed. São Paulo: Bushatsky, 1977.

FABRETTI, Láudio Camargo and Dilene Ramos. *Tax Law for Business Administration and Accounting Courses.* São Paulo: Atlas, 1999.

FABRETTI, Láudio Camargo and Dilene Ramos. *Tax Law for Business Administration and Accounting Courses. 2.* ed. São Paulo: Atlas, 2002.

FERNANDES, José Luiz Nunes. Tax planning: truths and uncertainties. In: CONGRESSO BRASILEIRO DE CONTABILIDADE, XVI, 2000, Goiânia: Conselho Federal de Contabilidade, Tema 8 : A contabilidade e a tributação. Available at http://www.quiadotrc.com.br.

FIPECAFL *Manual of Corporate Accounting: applicable to other companies.* 7. ed. São Paulo: Atlas, 2007.

FOSSATI, Gustavo. *Tax Planning and Economic Interpretation.*
Porto Alegre: Livraria do Advogado, 2006.

GIL, Antonio Carlos. *How to prepare research projects.* 4. ed. São Paulo: Atlas, 2002.

HIGUCHI, Hiromi; HIGUCHI, Celso Hiroyuki; HIGUCHI, Fábio Hiroshi. *Corporate Income Tax - Interpretation and Practice.* 6. ed. São Paulo: IR Publicações Ltda, 2006.

HACK, Érico. *Tax Law.* Curitiba, Iesde, 2008.

HUCK, Hermes Marcelo. *Evasion and Elision.* São Paulo: Saraiva, 1997.

http://www.portaltributario.com.br, 2018)

IBPT- Brazilian Institute of Tax Planning - Distributed handout Training for Tax Professionals 2009.

IUDÍCIBUS, Sérgio MARION, José Carlos. *Commercial Accounting.* 8. ed. São Paulo : Atlas, 2009.

LATORRACA, Nilton. *Tax Law: Corporate Income Tax* - Updated to 31-12-1999 by Rutnéa Navarro Guerreiro and Sérgio Murilo Zaloma Latorraca. 15. ed. São Paulo. Atlas, 2000.

MORAES, Bernardo Ribeiro de. *Compendium of Tax Law,* v.1., 2. ed. Rio de Janeiro: Forense, 1993.

NEVES, Silvério das; VICECONTI, Paulo E. V. *Curso Prático de Imposto de Renda - Pessoa Jurídica e Tributos Conexos.* São Paulo: Atlas. 2007.

NOGUEIRA, R.B. Curso de Direito Tributário. 14. ed. São Paulo: Saraiva, 1995.

PEREIRA, Evarley dos Santos - Calculation of Real Profit in SPED - Advisory Trainee, Version 02. 2009.

RIANI, Flávio. *Public Sector Economics - An introductory approach.* Rio de Janeiro: LTC, 2009.

SOUZA, M.V. G. *Elisão e Evasão Fiscal. Boletim Jurídico,* Uberaba/MG, a. 3, n. 127. Available at: <http://www.boletimjuridico.com.br/doutrina/texto.asp?id=636>. Accessed on: 12 Nov 2009.

SILVA, José Afonso da. *Course in Positive Constitutional Law.* 17. ed. São Paulo: Malheiros Editores, 2000.

SOUZA, Rubens Gomes de. *Compendium of Tax Legislation. 4.* ed. posthumous - São Paulo: Resenha Tributária, 1982.

VALÉRIO, Walter Paldes. *Tax Law Programme.* General Part. 5. ed. Porto Alegre: Sulina, 1978

XAVIER, Alberto. *International Tax Law of Brazil.* 4. ed. Rio de Janeiro: Forense, 1995.

ANNEX I

TRIAL BALANCE OF THE PROFIT AND LOSS ACCOUNTS FOR 2017 OF CIA SILAS SANCHES

	DEBIT	CREDIT	BALANCE
EXPENSES	39.081.584,32D	19.211.384,63	19.870.199,69D
OPERATING EXPENSES	38.731.692,91 D	19.200.201,32	19.531.491,59D
OPERATING EXPENSES	37.364.527,14D	19.100.201,32	18.264.325,82D
PERSONNEL COSTS	12.985.900,98D	165.101,89	12.820.799,09D
DIRECT INCOME	520.380,55D	0,00	520.380,55D
Board fees	415.127,11D	0,00	415.127,11D
Statutory bonus	11.289.32D	0,00	11.289.32D

Board holidays	55.367,29D	0,00	55.367,29D
Thirteenth Salary	38.596,83D	0,00	38.596,83D
SOCIAL CHARGES DIRECTORATE	153.417,60D	0,00	153.417,60D
INSS - National Social Security Institute	84.678,12D	0,00	84.678,12D
Education Salary	8.385,82D	0,00	8.385,82D
FGTS - Severance Indemnity Fund	26.834,50D	0,00	26.834,50D
INSS on holidays	13.978,41 D	0,00	13.978,41 D
FGTS without holidays	4.429,35D	0,00	4.429,35D
INSS s/13 Salary	9.674,61 D	0,00	9.674,61 D
FGTS s/13 Salary	3.087,70D	0,00	3.087,70D
Education Salary s/Holidays	1.384.24D	0,00	1.384.24D
Education Salary s/13	964,85D	0,00	964,85D
PERSONAL INCOME	7.387.672,89D	65.335,53	7.322.337,36D
Salaries	4.702.598,70D	5.155,41	4.697.443,29D
Gratuities	422.547,45D	0,00	422.547,45D
Overtime	211.954.34D	0,00	211.954.34D
Additional night	38.808,19D	0,00	38.808,19D
Thirteenth Salary	555.712,00D	9.653,24	546.058,76D
Biennium/Five-year period	649.039,64D	0,00	649.039,64D
Holiday provision	789.638,69D	2.284,62	787.354,07D
Hazardous/unhealthy working conditions	12.373,67D	0,00	12.373,67D
Recup. Expenses Income	17.03D	15.302,56	15.285,53C
Recup. Holiday expenses	0,00	32.939,70	32.939,70C
Prior notice of employment	4.983,18D	0,00	4.983,18D
PERSONNEL SOCIAL CHARGES	2.702.521,73D	82.217,81	2.620.303,92D
INSS National Social Security Institute	1.585.888,61D	0,00	1.585.888,61D
Education Salary	163.489,59D	0,00	163.489,59D
FGTS Guarantee Fund	487.294,38D	0,00	487.294,38D
Recup. INSS Expenses	0,00	48.963,99	48.963,99C
Recup. Education Salary Expenses	0,00	13.201,32	13.201,32C
Recup. FGTS Expenses	92,66D	18.985,12	18.892,46C
INSS on holidays	198.446,82D	578,01	197.868,81 D
FGTS on holidays	59.786,96D	182,77	59.604,19D
INSS s/13 Salary	133.151,54D	63,82	133.087,72D
FGTS s/13 Salary	42.228,88D	20,18	42.208,70D
Education salary without holidays	18.946,48D	216,29	18.730,19D
Education salary s/13 salary	13.195,81D	6,31	13.189,50D
OTHER INCOME	2.221.908,21 D	17.548,55	2.204.359,66D
Remuneration of the Supervisory Board	45.443,94D	0,00	45.443,94D
Remuneration of the Board of Directors	77.234,10D	0,00	77.234,10D
Funeral allowance	19.251,84D	0,00	19.251,84D
Travel Life Insurance	14.114,31D	0,00	14.114,31D
Social and Medical Assistance	311.260,79D	0,00	311.260.79D
Snacks Employee meals	179.747,45D	0,00	179.747,45D
Trainee Support	150.704,05D	0,00	150.704,05D
Instruction and Training	38.115,95D	1.436,95	36.679,00D
Miles Travelled	50,60D	0,00	50.60D
Accommodation	63.254,43D	0,00	63.254,43D
Food vouchers	912.228,76D	580,23	911.648.53D
Transport vouchers	173.162,89D	1.064,59	172.098,30D
Daily Allowance	57.243,31 D	7.869,22	49.374,09D
Travelling Surplus	65.163,65D	336,22	64.827,43D
Employee transport	94.211,26D	0,00	94.211.26D
Recup. Food voucher expenses	0,00	4.047,76	4.047,76C
Recup. Transport expenses	0,00	1.417,24	1.417,24C
Recover. Expenses Other Income	28,00D	796,34	768,34C
Holiday Allowance	4.519,12D	0,00	4.519,12D
Employee day-care centre agreement	16.173,76D	0,00	16.173,76D
EXPENDITURE ON MATERIALS	1.486.824,53D	3.172,13	1.483.652,40D
MATERIALS	1.486.824,53D	3.172,13	1.483.652,40D
Uniforms	52.200,53D	0,00	52.200,53D
Fuels and Lubricants	124.601,70D	0,00	124.601,70D
Office hours	239.530,33D	213,03	239.317,30D

Maintenance Dependency Maintenance	328.503,52D	10,60	328.492,92D
Maintenance Vehicle Maintenance	44.067,07D	783,58	43.283,49D
Maintenance Telecoms Equipment	1.935,74D	2,47	1.933.27D
Maintenance Other Assets	28.674,95D	0,00	28.674,95D
Maintenance Furniture and . Utensils	1.434,75D	0,00	1.434.75D
Maintenance Streets and Gardens	25.473,77D	0,00	25.473,77D
Maintenance Machinery and Equipment	34.088,62D	0,00	34.088,62D
Maintenance Installations	157.171,32D	297,27	156.874,05D
Miscellaneous Consumables	80.130,53D	0,00	80.130,53D
Cleaning	127.464,89D	0,00	127.464.89D
Security	5.713,82D	0,00	5.713,82D
Permanent Assets	658,90D	0,00	658,90D
Technology, IT and Systems	56.347,80D	170,73	56.177.07D
Recovery Maintenance Dependence	0,00	1.694,45	1.694.45C
Books Magazines and Newspapers	4.822,50D	0,00	4.822,50D
Indeductible Expenses	39.034,13D	0,00	39.034,13D
Gas	13.981,40D	0,00	13.981,40D
Cup and kitchen utensils	42.292,00D	0,00	42.292,00D
Promotion and Events	78.696,26D	0,00	78.696,26D
SERVICE AND INSURANCE COSTS	21.113.022,36D	8.029.724,80	13.083.297,56D
SERVICE	21.113.022,36D	8.029.724,80	13.083.297,56D
Electricity and Gas	8.463.215,27D	53.507,40	8.409.707,87D
Telephone	269.318,59D	0,00	269.318,59D
Water and Sewage	2.432.144,80D	235.503,23	2.196.641,57D
Books Magazines and Newspapers	17.812,22D	0,00	17.812,22D
Legal Advertising	113.337,78D	0,00	113.337,78D
Air and Road Tickets	208.110.29D	12.650,21	195.460,08D
Urban Driving	54.978,91 D	190,90	54.788,01 D
Freight Movements	1.537.79D	0,00	1.537.79D
Copies Authentications and Revelations	5.739,12D	0,00	5.739,12D
Rents and Condominiums	85.585,99D	0,00	85.585,99D
Bookbinding	771.00D	0,00	771.00D
Post and Telegraph	15.028,00D	0,00	15.028,00D
Professional Technical Services	3.295.178,31 D	12.159,48	3.283.018,83D
Studies and Projects	87.065,27D	0,00	87.065,27D
Courier services	30.471,01D	0,00	30.471,01D
Third party snacks and meals	131.906.19D	0,00	131.906.19D
Maintenance Vehicles	24.544,11 D	397,52	24.146.59D
Maintenance Dependencies	777.941,00D	459,63	777.481,37D
Maintenance Fixtures and Fittings	860,00D	0,00	860,00D
Maintenance Equipment Telecoms	90.00D	0,00	90.00D
Maintenance Installations	15.178.26D	0,00	15.178.26D
Maintenance Machinery and Equipment	45.380,58D	0,00	45.380,58D
Maintenance Streets and Gardens	15.192.49D	0,00	15.192.49D
Parking and tolls	2.388,10D	0,00	2.388,10D
Technology, IT and Systems	88.163.07D	0,00	88.163.07D
Vehicle Insurance	14.409,88D	0,00	14.409,88D
Institutional publicity	414.073,60D	2.200,00	411.873.60D
Equipment Hire	105.397,76D	2.334,40	103.063,36D
Consultancy and Auditing	328.755,65D	0,00	328.755,65D
General Services	314.733,95D	41,70	314.692,25D
Recovery Electricity Costs	5.032,09D	7.339.983,17	7.334.951,08C
Recup. Water and Sewerage	0,00	226.034,50	226.034,50C
Recovery Maintenance Dependency	0,00	3.981,24	3.981,24C
Recovery Phones	0,00	15.461,23	15.461,23C
Recovery Professional Technical Services	0,00	15.523,59	15.523,59C
Recovery General Services Expenses	0,00	10.341,62	10.341,62C
Recup. Studies and Projects	0,00	275,00	275,00C
Recovery Rent and Condominium Expenses	0,00	7.066,29	7.066,29C
Car Hire	6.833,09D	0,00	6.833,09D
Guard and surveillance	1.785.780,74D	0,00	1.785.780,74D
Recovery Guard and surveillance expenses	0,00	20.921,28	20.921,28C
Recup. Snacks and Meals	0,00	63.142,41	63.142,41 C
Disclosure	210,00D	0,00	210,00D
Sponsorship	13.533,38D	0,00	13.533,38D

Cleaning Service	1.431.292,07D	0,00	1.431.292,07D
Composting Organic Material	229.100,91 D	0,00	229.100,91 D
Property Insurance	42,78D	0,00	42,78D
Common Expenses - RDC	63.731,66D	0,00	63.731,66D
SISBACEN Information	5.831,73D	0,00	5.831,73D
Promotion and Events	212.324,92D	7.550,00	204.774,92D
DEPRECIATION AND AMORTISATION	953.416,24D	0,03	953.416,21 D
DEPRECIATION AND AMORTISATION	953.416,24D	0,03	953.416,21 D
Depreciation and Amortisation	637.666,73D	0,03	637.666,70D
Depreciation and Amortisation Law 10865/04	311.675,11 D	0,00	311.675,11 D
Depreciation IPC/1990 - Value in Use	4.074,40D	0,00	4.074,40D
RECOVERY OF COMMON EXPENSES	825.363,03D	10.902.202,47	10.076.839,44C
RECOVERY OF OF COMMON EXPENSES	825.363,03D	10.902.202,47	10.076.839,44C
App. Common Expenses - Counting	671.698,25D	9.656.802,15	8.985.103,90C
Appeal of Common Expenses - Uberlândia	116.281,20D	541.140,88	424.859,68C
Common Appeal - Juiz de Fora	12.675,07D	185.757,71	173.082,64C
Common Charges - G. Valadares	19.785,95D	227.832,00	208.046,05C
Calculation of Common Expenses - Caratinga	4.922,56D	88.159,58	83.237,02C
Appeal of Common Expenses - Barbacena	0,00	202.510,15	202.510,15C
PROVISION FOR OPERATING EXPENSES	1.367.165,77D	100.000,00	1.267.165,77D
PROVISION FOR OPERATING EXPENSES	1.367.165,77D	100.000,00	1.267.165,77D
PROVISION FOR OPERATING EXPENSES	1.367.165,77D	100.000,00	1.267.165,77D
Provisions Civil Contingencies	500.000,00D	0,00	500.000,00D
Labour provisions	250.000,00D	100.000,00	150.000,00D
Tax and civil provisions	49.019,89D	0,00	49.019,89D
Provision for Doubtful Debts	568.145,88D	0,00	568.145,88D
TAX AND DUTY EXPENSES	149.538,64D	10.923,31	138.615,33D
TAX AND DUTY EXPENSES	149.538,64D	10.923,31	138.615,33D
TAXES AND CHARGES	149.538,64D	10.923,31	138.615,33D
TAXES AND CHARGES	149.538,64D	10.923,31	138.615,33D
Miscellaneous Taxes and Fees	33.366,89D	5.110,81	28.256,08D
Legal and Judicial Expenses	43.100,80D	0,00	43.100,80D
IPVA	13.628,70D	0,00	13.628,70D
CPMF	2.689,79D	0,00	2.689,79D
Employer's Union Contribution	18.298,99D	0,00	18.298,99D
Recovery of expenses. Miscellaneous Taxes and Fees	0,00	5.812,50	5.812,50C
INSS Third parties	32.723,64D	0,00	32.723,64D
Urban Land Tax - IPTU	5.729,83D	0,00	5.729,83D
FINANCIAL EXPENSES	62.899,74D	79,00	62.820,74D
FINANCIAL EXPENSES	62.899,74D	79,00	62.820,74D
FINANCIAL	62.899,74D	79,00	62.820,74D
FINANCIAL	62.899,74D	79,00	62.820,74D
Monetary Variation Liabilities	49.817,99D	0,00	49.817,99D
Bank charges	4.267,83D	79,00	4.188.83D
Interest Liabilities	947,97D	0,00	947,97D
Discounts granted	1.189.40D	0,00	1.189.40D
Late payment penalty	3.554,35D	0,00	3.554,35D
Present Value Adjustment	2.832,68D	0,00	2.832,68D
IOF	289,28D	0,00	289,28D
Other Operating Expenses	0,24D	0,00	0,24D
OTHER EXPENSES	25.729,90D	0,00	25.729,90D
OTHER EXPENSES	25.729,90D	0,00	25.729,90D
CONTRIBUTIONS AND DONATIONS	25.729,90D	0,00	25.729,90D
CONTRIBUTIONS AND DONATIONS	25.729,90D	0,00	25.729,90D
Trade association	19.429,90D	0,00	19.429,90D

Expenses Agreements	6.300,00D	0,00	6.300,00D
OTHER EXPENSES	111.723.13D	181,00	111.542.13D
OTHER EXPENSES	111.723.13D	181,00	111.542.13D
EXTRAORDINARY	111.723.13D	181,00	111.542.13D
EXTRAORDINARY	111.723.13D	181,00	111.542.13D
Inventory Adjustment	181.00D	181,00	0,00
Capital losses	8.962,37D	0,00	8.962,37D
School-Creche Agreement	9.549,76D	0,00	9.549,76D
Agreements	92.400,00D	0,00	92.400,00D
Indeductible Infringement	630,00D	0,00	630,00D
REVENUE	2.339.408,38D	26.126.466,88	23.787.058,50C
GROSS OPERATING REVENUE	2.329.700,29D	24.577.823,19	22.248.122,90C
GROSS OPERATING REVENUE	2.329.700,29D	24.577.823,19	22.248.122,90C
GROSS OPERATING REVENUE	2.329.700,29D	24.577.823,19	22.248.122,90C
SERVICES	38.297,05D	24.020.028,04	23.981.730,99C
Use Fee - Boxes	0,00	13.887.324,19	13.887.324,19C
Subletting Revenue Boxes	0,00	254.308,22	254.308,22C
Weighing	332,00D	212.599,00	212.267,00C
Charger/Cap Register	0,00	4.924,00	4.924,00C
Various recipes	0,03D	1,33	1,30C
Accommodation/Producer's Lodge	2.613,00D	164.010,77	161.397.77C
Street vendors	176,00D	59.592,00	59.416,00C
CSV - Commercialisation of Vehicles	2.017,56D	426.278,61	424.261,05C
Publicity	0,00	18.480,00	18.480,00C
Administration income	0,00	820.256,35	820.256,35C
Transfer Fee	639,43D	1.469.523,04	1.468.883,61C
Modules	6.642,20D	1.807.934,46	1.801.292,26C
Car park	30,00D	59.905,00	59.875,00C
Hire of trolleys	148,00D	18.706,00	18.558,00C
Wholesaler	0,00	106.070,00	106.070,00C
Fixed Banking	0,00	3.847,00	3.847,00C
Snack Bar	0,00	12.320,00	12.320,00C
Producer Registration	163,00D	92.467,00	92.304,00C
Charger Monthly fee	292,00D	147.719,00	147.427.00C
Certificate of Origin	33.00D	51.127,00	51.094.00C
Single Certificate of Origin	222,00D	20.179,00	19.957.00C
Special Certificate of Origin	0,00	146,00	146.00C
Leafy Merchant Modules	133,39D	12.284,00	12.150.61C
Green Area Exhibition	0,00	28.445,00	28.445.00C
Fixed Preferential Credential Module	0,00	87.366,36	87.366.36C
Monthly Fixed Module	0,00	444.402,63	444.402.63C
Modulo S/ Fixed Preferential Credential	0,00	90.814,52	90.814.52C
Permanence Area Fortnightly 49/50	0,00	285,00	285,00C
Stay Monthly Area 01/48	270,00D	25.945,00	25.675,00C
Special stay	0,00	36.262,23	36.262,23C
Standard stay	344,00D	2.104,00	1.760.00C
Credential renewal	208,00D	20.320,50	20.112.50C
Romaneio Entry	234,00D	66.680,50	66.446.50C
Single Entry Romaneio	0,00	427,00	427,00C
Tender Processes	22.406,29D	2.427.248,01	2.404.841,72C
Single retailer	0,00	14.962,00	14.962,00C
Retail Mensalista	0,00	96.950,00	96.950,00C
Business Rates	60,00D	101.377,67	101.317.67C
Bucket 1	0,00	2.356,00	2.356.00C
Bucket 2	0,00	1.142,00	1.142.00C
Shops Employee Registration	0,00	44.668,00	44.668.00C
Car Wash	0,00	2.215,00	2.215.00C
Stay Standard Area 266/301 01/32	0,00	32.929,00	32.929.00C
Temporary stay	624,00D	23.801,00	23.177.00C
Technical reserve	709,15D	818.833,65	818.124.50C
Retail register	0,00	491,00	491.00C

DEDUCTIONS FROM GROSS REVENUE	2.291.403,24D	557.795,15	1.733.608,09D
(-) PASEP	395.470,56D	0,00	395.470,56D
(-) COFINS	1.821.561,36D	0,00	1.821.561,36D
(-) Cancelled Services and Discounts Inc.	74.371,32D	0,00	74.371,32D
PASEP Recovery - Tax Credit	0,00	99.498,59	99.498,59C
Cofins Recovery - Tax Credit	0,00	458.296,56	458.296,56C
RECOVERY AND REVERSAL	0,00	60.552,83	60.552,83C
RECOVERY AND REVERSAL	0,00	60.552,83	60.552,83C
RECOVERY REVERSAL EXPENSES	0,00	60.552,83	60.552,83C
RECOVERY REVERSAL EXPENSES	0,00	60.552,83	60.552,83C
Recovery Legal Expenses	0,00	438,52	438,52C
Recovery Copies Authentications	0,00	556,95	556,95C
Recup. Expenses for Surveillance Services	0,00	59.557,36	59.557,36C
FINANCIAL INCOME	9.708,09D	1.305.448,55	1.295.740,46C
FINANCIAL INCOME	9.708,09D	1.305.448,55	1.295.740,46C
FINANCIAL	9.708,09D	1.305.448,55	1.295.740,46C
FINANCIAL	9.708,09D	1.305.448,55	1.295.740,46C
Interest Assets	670,10D	95.683,88	95.013,78C
Dividends Received	0,00	42.723,34	42.723,34C
Contractual fines	4.329,43D	168.984,49	164.655,06C
Income from Securities	3.849,81 D	760.371,95	756.522,14C
Monetary Variations in Assets	544,75D	192.086,60	191.541.85C
Discounts obtained	0,00	19.415,79	19.415,79C
Notice of Infringement -1	0,00	9.145,00	9.145.00C
Material Release	0,00	840,00	840,00C
Product Release	0,00	1.549,50	1.549.50C
Release of seized trolleys	314,00D	14.648,00	14.334,00C
OTHER INCOME	0,00	182.642,31	182.642,31 C
OTHER INCOME	0,00	182.642,31	182.642,31 C
EXTRAORDINARY	0,00	182.642,31	182.642,31 C
EXTRAORDINARY	0,00	182.642,31	182.642,31 C
Eventual Income	0,00	75.767,07	75.767,07C
Capital Gains	0,00	106.875,24	106.875,24C
CALCULATING THE RESULT	1.673.623,26D	20.177,41	1.653.445,85D
RESULT FOR THE YEAR	1.673.623,26D	20.177,41	1.653.445,85D
RESULT FOR THE YEAR	1.673.623,26D	20.177,41	1.653.445,85D
CALCULATION OF THE RESULT FOR THE YEAR	1.673.623,26D	20.177,41	1.653.445,85D
RESULT FOR THE YEAR	134.386,66D	0,00	134.386,66D
Accounting Results	134.386,66D	0,00	134.386,66D
CORPORATE INCOME TAX	1.120.134,71D	20.177,41	1.099.957,30D
Income Tax	1.120.134,71D	20.177,41	1.099.957,30D
SOCIAL CONTRIBUTION ON PROFIT	419.101,89D	0,00	419.101,89D
Social Contribution on Profits	419.101,89D	0,00	419.101,89D
TOTAL DEBTS:	468.112,28D		
TOTAL CREDITS:	468.112,28C		

Abbreviations: Manut. (maintenance), Cons. (conservation), Recup. (recovery) Desp.(expense)

Source: Balance Sheet of Cia Silas Sanches S/A as at 31/12/2017

MIX
Papier aus verantwortungsvollen Quellen
Paper from responsible sources
FSC® C105338

Printed by Books on Demand GmbH, Norderstedt / Germany